The Politics of Successful Governance Reforms

This book examines the factors that give rise to successful governance reforms in developing countries, focusing on the importance of political commitment, supportive institutions, and the timing of reforms. It reviews the lessons arising from the design and implementation of successful governance reforms in Brazil, India, Uganda and other parts of Africa through comparative analysis of experience with public financial management, anti-corruption, civil service reform, and innovations in service delivery.

The contributors suggest that three factors are critical in explaining positive outcomes:

- strong, consistent commitment from politicians to initiate and sustain reforms;
- a high level of technical capacity and some degree of insulation from societal interests, at least in the early phases, for designing and managing reforms;
- incremental approaches with cumulative benefits are more likely to produce sustainable results.

Explicit attention to the political feasibility of reform, identifying and building incentives for reform, and a more gradual and piecemeal approach are all integral to the success of future governance reforms.

This book was published as a special issue of *Commonwealth and Comparative Politics*.

Mark Robinson is Head of Profession for Governance and Conflict at the UK Department for International Development. At the time of the study he was Team Leader of the Governance Team at the Institute of Development Studies.

The Politics of Successful Governance Reforms

Edited by Mark Robinson

Routledge
Taylor & Francis Group

LONDON AND NEW YORK

First published 2009 by Routledge
2 Park Square, Milton Park, Abingdon, Oxon, OX14 4RN

Simultaneously published in the USA and Canada
by Routledge
270 Madison Avenue, New York, NY 10016

Routledge is an imprint of the Taylor & Francis Group, an informa business

© 2009 Edited by Mark Robinson

Typeset in Times by Value Chain, India
Printed and bound in Great Britain by MPG Books Ltd, Bodmin, Cornwall

British Library Cataloguing in Publication Data
A catalogue record for this book is available from the British Library

ISBN 10: 0-415-44569-8
ISBN 13: 978-0-415-44569-6

Contents

ACKNOWLEDGEMENTS

This volume draws together papers originally prepared for a study commissioned by the Public Sector Governance Group in the Poverty Reduction and Economic Management Network of the World Bank. We are especially grateful to Poul Engberg-Pedersen, currently Director General of the Norwegian Agency for International Cooperation, who initiated this research as senior public sector governance specialist at the World Bank. We are also grateful to other members of the Public Sector Governance Group, notably Ed Campos, Phil Keefer, Sanjay Pradhan and Randi Ryterman for their comments on earlier versions of the chapters.

The authors would also like to acknowledge the support and advice received from a number of people during the course of fieldwork. In Brazil they include Fernando Blanco, Yasuhiko Matsuda, Selena Nunes, Jose Roberto Afonso, Paulo Mauricio Teixeira Da Costa, and Jose Guilherme Reis. For the India study, we would particularly like to thank Stephen Howes and B.P.R. Vithal in the World Bank office in New Delhi, Jos Mooij and Jayaprakash Narayan in Hyderabad, Samuel Paul, M.R. Sreenivasa Murthy and Narendar Pani in Bangalore, and Jonathan Caseley and Narayana Gatty at the Institute of Development Studies. In Uganda, we would like to thank Grace Yabrudy and Sudharshan Canagarajah, respectively Country Manager and Senior Economist in the World Bank office in Kampala at the time of the study.

Finally, we are grateful to Sinnet Weber and Judy Hartley for formatting and copy-editing the final drafts.

NOTES ON CONTRIBUTORS

Anne Marie Goetz is Chief Advisor for Governance, Peace and Security at UNIFEM. Prior to joining UNIFEM in 2005, she was a Professor of Political Science at the Institute of Development Studies, University of Sussex. She is the author of six books on the subjects of gender and politics in developing countries, and on accountability reforms, including *Governing Women: Women in Politics and Governance in Development* (2006), and *Reinventing Accountability: Making Democracy Work for Human Development* (Palgrave, 2005) (co-authored with Rob Jenkins).

Brian Levy currently is Adviser for Public Sector Governance in the World Bank. He is the author of *Governance Reform: Bridging Monitoring and Action* (World Bank, 2007), which builds on his 2006 work on governance monitoring featured in the 2006 Global Monitoring Report, *Mutual Accountability: Aid, Trade and Governance*. He has published numerous books and articles on the interactions between public institutions, the private sector and development in Africa, East Asia, and elsewhere, most recently editing (jointly with Sahr Kpundeh) the volume, *Building State Capacity in Africa* (World Bank Institute, 2004).

James Manor is the Emeka Anyaoku Professor in the Institute of Commonwealth Studies, University of London. He previously taught at Yale, Harvard and Leicester Universities, at the Institute of Development Studies, University of Sussex and the Institute for Social and Economic Change, Bangalore, India. Forthcoming books include E. Raghavan and J. Manor, *Transforming Politics in Karnataka: Democracy Broadened, Deepened, Entrenched*, and M. A. Melo, N. Ng'ethe and J. Manor, *Against the Odds: Politicians, Institutions and the Struggle against Poverty*.

Mark Robinson is Head of Profession for Governance and Conflict at the UK Department for International Development. He previously held appointments as Fellow and Governance Team Leader at the Institute of Development Studies, University of Sussex, and as Research Fellow for the Overseas Development in London. Mark also served as Program Officer for Governance and Civil Society in the New Delhi office of the Ford Foundation. He has published extensively on democratisation, governance, and civil society and most recently edited *Budgeting for the Poor: Civil Society, Transparency and Accountability* (Palgrave Macmillan, forthcoming).

Aaron Schneider is Assistant Professor of Political Science and Latin American studies at Tulane University, New Orleans. He specialises in development and public finance, with a particular interest on the way in which changing international market processes are accommodated within national political structures.

Introduction: The Politics of Successful Governance Reforms

MARK ROBINSON

Achieving success in governance reform is challenging in the best of circumstances. Experience of reforms designed to improve the accountability and effectiveness of public institutions has been very mixed and the reasons behind their failure are well established. Governance reforms typically founder on account of political factors, rooted in a combination of inadequate political commitment and considerable political resistance. Such reforms run into political problems because they challenge the balance of political power by increasing accountability of politicians and reducing the scope for discretion on the part of public officials. Governance reforms also run into difficulties on account of excessive ambition, short time horizons and inadequate administrative capacity. The challenge for research is to identify the circumstances in which developing country governments successfully design and implement governance reforms.

The papers published in this issue have their origins in two comparative research exercises sponsored by the World Bank. One study, led by the Governance Team at the Institute of Development Studies, set out to explain the factors that underpin successful governance reforms through comparative case studies in Brazil, India and Uganda. These centred on analysing the political and institutional variables that shaped positive governance reform outcomes in the three countries, through a comparison of reforms in the civil service, public financial management, tax administration, anti-corruption and service delivery. While the reforms varied in scope, duration and ambition they all shared the objective of improving the accountability, probity and effectiveness of public sector institutions. Five of the papers draw on research from this study. The second research exercise focused on comparative experience of reforms designed to improve state capacity in sub-Saharan Africa. The main findings are summarised in a single synthesis paper.

The six papers that comprise this volume are presented in the following order. The collection begins with a paper by Anne Marie Goetz that sketches out a conceptual framework for analysing successful governance reforms. This is followed by James Manor's review of successful innovations in service delivery in the Indian states of Andhra Pradesh and Karnataka. The trajectories of three types of governance reform in Uganda – civil service reform, tax administration and anti-corruption – are analysed in the subsequent paper by Mark Robinson. Aaron Schneider's paper on fiscal reforms in Brazil comes next, centred on two contrasting case studies of reforms in federal taxation and public financial management. Brian Levy's paper synthesises the findings of research on reforms aimed at strengthening state capacity in a number of African countries.

The issue ends with a summary paper that captures the salient features of successful governance reforms in Brazil, India and Uganda, highlighting the importance of three particular factors: sustained political commitment, a high level of bureaucratic capacity, and a gradual approach to reform characterised by cumulative initiatives over an extended period of time. Similar lessons are highlighted by Levy from his review of sub-Saharan African experience in which successful reforms are found to result from the incentives that motivate decision-makers and incremental approaches to reform implementation. The insights from this research have implications for the design of governance reforms elsewhere: achieving positive results depends on the political feasibility of reform, the scope to build political incentives for reform, and the willingness of politicians and bureaucrats to champion a sustained reform agenda.

Manoeuvring Past Clientelism: Institutions and Incentives to Generate Constituencies in Support of Governance Reforms

ANNE MARIE GOETZ

Institute of Development Studies, Sussex University

Introduction

Most governance reforms fail (Polidano, 2001). They fail not for a want of top-level 'political will', though this is the most often invoked cause of failure. Most developing country leaders today genuinely endorse efforts to reduce corruption, improve state capacity, and deliver services more efficiently and effectively. Governance reforms often fail, however, because they tend to threaten existing power relations: the patronage systems through which political advantage is maintained, the patterns of collusion through which public resources are diverted to favoured groups. The considerable political consensus and technical skill needed to subvert these systems is often wanting in states that lack the social reach of their advanced counterparts, and in governments that do not enjoy a broad mandate.

This article offers a framework for the study of the political and institutional conditions at that may support governance reforms. The reforms considered here are intended to improve public expenditure management, the delivery of services and the promotion of accountability. Detailed in-country research into the lessons that can be drawn from the design and implementation of governance reforms is found in the case studies of Brazil, the Indian states of Karnataka and Andhra Pradesh, and Uganda in this collection.

This conceptual framework identifies aspects of institutional change upon which we should focus when seeking to understand why in any particular case reformers have been able to generate support for good governance. These considerations are drawn from a wide range of analyses of the politics of reform. These include the large literature on the political economy of economic adjustment,[1] literature on the politics of democratisation,[2] on developmental states,[3] new work on imperfections in political markets,[4] literature on corruption and politics,[5] and on the politics of contemporary Poverty Reduction Strategy (PRS) processes.[6] Propositions concerning the importance of particular institutional developments or political processes are also based on analyses of the successes and failures of donor-supported administrative and accountability reforms.[7]

This article suggests that two major incentives drive politicians when weighing up reform options: first, the incentive to maintain (or not threaten) tried and tested existing patterns of support (often based on patronage systems); second, the incentive to generate new sources of support or political alliances. These incentives are in turn determined by formal and informal political institutions, by the nature of connections between the state and civil society through which buy-in to reform is arranged, and by the sheer political skill of reform-minded leaders.

Reform involves considerable risk to leaders: risk that they will lose patronage resources (public sector jobs and rents), and also lose popular support. Factors that influence the capacity of reformers to take political risks in undercutting the privileges of elites accustomed to seeking rents through the state or that enable reformers to generate support from groups likely to benefit from reform are divided, in this article, between structural features of politics and society that determine adaptability of social institutions to change, and features of the reform process itself that shape the location, intensity, and the target of the 'shock' of reform. These features include sequencing, technical capacity of the public administration, levels of government at which reform is pursued, and the monitorability of reform.

Under certain conditions, which we describe for each of these institutional or reform design variables, the perceived risk of reform can be reduced, and reform can become more attractive to politicians keen to stay in power and to take credit for results.

Definitions

'*Governance*' is described by the World Bank as 'the manner in which the State exercises and acquires authority' (Campos & Pradhan, 2003: 1). 'Good' governance brings in normative judgements about what constitutes the legitimate acquisition, and efficient and equitable exercise of power. For some donor agencies, good governance therefore implies *democratic* governance. Definitions of good governance thus diverge between a restricted view that identifies good governance with sound management of the economy, and a more expansive one that embraces political liberalisation, and addresses democratic deficits, including problems of social inequality (Santiso, 2001: 4).[8]

This article addresses what have been described as 'second generation' reforms, following a first reform generation of economic stabilisation, designed to relax the state's grip on the market. Second-generation reforms are intended to promote structural changes in state institutions, particularly the political institutions in charge of economic policy formulation, implementation and oversight (Naim, 1995). These include institutional reforms that over the long term can contribute to better macroeconomic management (independent central banks, autonomous tax boards), encourage economic growth (protections for private property, rule of law and enforcement of contracts), deliver services (results-oriented management in the public sector, improved budgeting and auditing, decentralisation), and ensure accountability (anti-corruption measures, merit-based recruitment in the public service, support to the oversight committees of parliament, judicial reform).

There is an expectation that governance reform will be most readily achieved in states open to economic and political liberalisation, where high-capacity bureaucracies can be insulated from social pressure and implement coherent policy delivered from government leaders. But to observe that good things go together does not indicate causation. Worse, it does not help to identify strategies to promote governance reform, because, as Caiden has observed, it appears that: '[C]ountries most in need of state reform are least able to implement it' (Caiden, 1994: 111). In other words, the capacity needed to reform economic management systems or accountability institutions requires reasonably developed bureaucracies in the first place. What is of interest to the governance agenda is the institutional framework in which policies are formulated. Which features of this institutional framework best support reform? This article applies itself to this question.

Analytical Framework: How Institutions Shape Incentives and Create Constituencies for Reform

The central dilemma that governance reforms pose to politicians inheres in their perceived high cost in terms of lost patronage resources, lost opportunities for private earnings, and an erosion of political support from public sector workers. Administrative reforms in particular decrease the ability of politicians to build political capital through the distribution of public sector appointments and jobs, or through the awarding of contracts. But engaging in governance reforms is not entirely irrational for politicians keen on political survival. Reforms can generate political pay-offs if they improve national economic performance, or if service delivery improvements generate support from voters (Geddes, 1991: 373). Under what conditions, then, will decision-makers opt to surrender their patronage methods and resources?

Explanatory frameworks for answering this question are found in rational choice theory, institutional economics and sociology, and comparative political economy. These approaches inform the proposition that the fate of governance reforms depends on how existing formal and informal institutions shape incentives for risk-taking in relation to reform, in contrast to the incentives they create for resisting reform and clinging to patronage systems.

Incentives for Reform: for Politicians

Two sets of incentives seem to trigger governance reform efforts in the first place, and then to ensure compliance. The first set applies to the apex power-holders and decision-makers who must take the first steps in setting up and sustaining credible reforms; the second set of incentives apply to the people who have to *implement* reforms. Political survival and reputation is the main incentive driving politicians and other decision-makers, thus reform often has to be constructed in such a way as to:

- *Not put an immediate end to rent-seeking or to old-style political deals.* From politicians' points of view, there is an incentive to reform if they know that reform does not spell an end of their ability to derive rents or other benefits (Jenkins, 1999: 83; Booth, 2003). They have an incentive to reform if they see some new source of funds to maintain their political careers, and also if they see that they can preserve their means of cultivating political support. The transition to multi-party politics in Ghana, according to Booth, has been much eased because politicians saw that they would easily be able to adapt pre-existing patronage systems to competitive politics (2003).
- *Create opportunities to cultivate new support groups and alliances.* Politicians will risk reform if they are confident that social groups will

respond creatively, rather than intransigently, new policies. And for politicians to feel confident of this, it helps if civil society is diverse and complex, and political freedoms to associate and articulate oppositional perspectives are secure.

Incentives for Reform: for Bureaucrats

The second set of incentives that must be considered are those animating the mid- and lower-level bureaucrats who must comply with reforms. A key practical constraint on governance reform is that while some of the most entrenched resistance to reform comes from the public administration, the public administration is also the key executing agency of reform, and its capacity limitations constitute a fundamental limit on the pace of reform. Reforms that tackle cost containment, organisational restructuring, fiscal hygiene, internal accountability systems have rarely been able to reduce incentives for corruption and moonlighting, and have tended to entrench bureaucratic resistance to reform.

Any systemic reform that threatens established means of doing business, and, more importantly, established channels of generating income, will be resisted or subverted by mid-level staff. Mid- and front-line state workers mediate relationships between the formal state institution that employs them, and the many informal institutions of which they are a part, and for which they are gate-keepers to unmerited access to state resources. A key incentive for changed behaviour on the part of these state workers is therefore not necessarily the (usually barely credible) threat of exposure and punishment, but rather, *an institutional survival alternative to patronage and rent-seeking*. State workers need not just a level of remuneration that rewards effort, but also a sense of mission, renewed professionalism, inspiration, and social status, enough status to offset the condemnation that will flow from refusing to favour their own specific social group.[9]

The following three elements of political institutions and competition in any context must be understood in order to frame an inquiry into the fate of governance reforms, because they shape the incentives facing politicians and public administrators:

(a) the formal and informal *political institutions* that shape choices made by public actors;

(b) the nature of the *connections between state and society* through which the compliance if not active support of non-state actors to reform is agreed (we pay particular attention to political parties and the nature of the party system, and to patronage relationships);

(c) the *political agency* required to package reforms, moderate their scope and pace, identify levels and arenas at which to begin, so that resistance is undermined.

Each is considered below:

(a) Institutions. The central importance of institutions inheres not only in their role in structuring relationships between governing elites and sectoral interests, but in their potential to shape incentives and react to changed circumstances in ways that can alter interest perceptions of various affected parties. A broad understanding of institutions is used here: sets of rules (these can be formally codified or informally understood) that shape roles and behaviours and expectations of social, political and economic actors (Hall & Taylor, 1996: 936).

Formal and informal institutions shape the way policy actors negotiate the political bargains that underwrite the sustainability of reform – i.e. – get buy-in from dissenters, and compensate losers (Jenkins, 1999). Electoral systems, intensity of political opposition, coalition versus majority governments, and the legislature's powers are features of the formal institutional environment that affect commitment to or sustainability of reform. An effective governance reform programme will have attempted to establish a sensible fit between these structural characteristics and reform ambitions. In the absence of a basic infrastructure of formal accountability, successful reforms will be modest and targeted narrowly on those institutions most amenable to change.

Often informal institutions are much more determinant of incentives and of the risk perceptions made by politicians or bureaucrats. Informal institutions are essential transmission belts between the state and civil society, and have the effect of generating support for reform, dissipating conflict, and compensating losers. We distinguish between formal and informal institutions on the basis of whether an institution is part of the formal state apparatus or not, and on the basis of the degree to which its rules and practices are codified and formalised. Informal institutions include associations built on ascriptive attachments (kin, clan, ethnic, or religion). Some observers argue that economic and governance reforms have increased the social influence of informal and non-governmental institutions, including the private sector, for instance through privatizing some state functions or enabling customary institutions (councils of elders, religious tribunals) to thrive because of the retraction of the state in some areas (Hibou, 2004).

While 'modern' informal institutions such as civil society groups and the media are supportive of accountability systems, 'traditional' informal institutions are often seen to have at least two damaging effects on governance. First, they undermine the incentives to political parties to make broad programmatic appeals to the electorate, encouraging instead narrowly focused promise-making and clientelist resource distribution. These informal institutions based on ethnicity or other ascriptive identities prevent poor clients of services from mobilising broadly on the basis of shared interests in better service provision. Instead the incentives are to fight each other in order to be the privileged recipients of targeted transfers. Second, loyalties and networks based on informal ascriptive institutions infuse public formal institutions, working at cross-purposes to formal incentive and accountability systems.

Informal institutions, unofficial loyalties and patterns of dispensing privilege are among the problems that governance reforms address, yet they also profoundly shape the outcomes that can be expected of governance reforms. Governance reforms have few tools to deal with informal institutions – the dominant approach is to hope that reform measures can gain a foothold in formal institutions before they are undermined by informal systems.

The critical role played by informal institutions is what prompts us to suggest that key incentives driving the adoption of reform are, first, the assurance that reform will not at least initially disrupt established operating patterns, including established patronage arrangements, and second, that reform holds out the chance of identifying and cultivating new sources of support and legitimacy.

(b) Connections between state and society. Structural reform requires more than just legislative action and the cooperation not only of line agencies and ministries, but also at least of some segments of society (Nelson, 1993: 438). Institutions to link state and society are essential to facilitate public oversight of governmental processes, and also to negotiate the new understandings or pacts that promote institutional change. In order to deflect, absorb, dissipate or compensate those who resist reform, reformers engage a range of formal and informal institutions – formal institutions such as forums for negotiating with public sector workers, or informal ones such as the patronage networks and ethnic loyalties or the range of civil society institutions to which political parties often have special access (Jenkins, 1999: 84). Institutions, formal and informal, that connect the government and citizens deserve special scrutiny for their role in mediating reforms. In highly centralised and closed systems of governance such as have characterised many African states it is precisely these connective institutions that are particularly weak (Barkan, 2000: 4) or have been co-opted by the state to extend dominant party control over rural citizens.

Political parties and their leaders are particularly key institutions for transmitting signals between the state and society. These institutions claim and often have a representativeness that many other non-state institutions lack. As Jenkins shows in his study of the politics of reform in India, parties preside over complex relationships established between leaders and a range of informal institutions, sometimes constituted as special interest groups, and these can galvanise support for or resistance to reform (1999). Where parties are poorly institutionalised and lack discipline (agreements struck with party leaders are not binding on the delegations of these parties, whose votes must be won one at a time, often through 'inducements', and who are prone to defection to other parties) the sheer cost of generating a coalition in support of reform rises, since it must be purchased first from a party's own members, then from other parties. Some observers feel this is precisely what delayed economic reform in Brazil in the 1980s and 1990s (Hagopian, 1998).

The programme orientation and discipline of political parties will be low where there is pervasive clientelism and segmented state corporatism – because state subsidies to different social groups create dependencies, and dissuade them from organising to demand national goals or to form broad coalitions (Weyland, 1994; Santiso, 2003). This has been the case in Brazil. Social groups try to advance their narrow interests through direct links to the state, not through parties. So parties are bypassed and excluded from crucial debates and decisions, and have limited importance. And since they have limited importance, they turn to clientelism for support. This undermines their capacity to serve as interest channels for the poor. Party systems become fragmented, as does civil society with multitudinous narrow interest groups pursuing special favours. This encourages politicians to focus on personal political survival to the neglect of collective goals.

In recent reviews of Poverty Reduction Strategy Paper (PRSP) exercises in Africa (Booth, 2003), and of new participatory public expenditure management experiments in Latin America (Brautigam, 2004), the absence of representative institutions (parties and trade unions) in many of these exercises is lamented. Brautigam comments that this is particularly unfortunate considering that a constant in all cases of effective pro-poor spending in Latin America has been the commitment of democratic and ideologically left-of-centre parties, which, regardless of whether they encouraged participatory decision-making, were able to fend off (or compensate) resistant elites and provide incentives to front-line state agents to deliver services to the poor (2004: 10–11).

When several reformist parties compete, the capture of poor voters is more difficult, and party credibility means that anti-poverty promises must be met. Arguably therefore, an institutional reform that is necessary for successful governance reforms is the removal of formal and informal barriers to free entry and exit from the party system.

The nature of political competition – the party system and the construction of majorities in the congress, parliament or national assembly – becomes salient when governments cannot advance reform through decree but must win legislative backing for it. Fragmented party systems, where a large number of parties compete (as in Brazil – 19 parties in 1990, 18 in 1994), or where large parties are highly factionalised, makes it difficult to build governing majorities in the constituent assembly, and this can undercut decisive reform action.

Historically the developmental successes and reform leaders amongst democracies have been those with dominant party systems (Botswana, Malaysia, Singapore, Mexico), in which one party has been continuously returned to power for extended periods. Is the same true for governance successes? Continuity creates incentives for reform-minded elites to unite rather than fragment, and to tackle reforms with extended maturity horizons – provided, of course, that they expect eventually to take credit for these reforms. Frequent changes of government or unstable coalitions restrict the focus of reformers on efforts with more immediate pay-offs. But intense competition between parties can impel politicians to improve governance and broaden the set of groups receiving benefits in order to win more votes next time. Long-established and vigorous competition with incumbent parties helps to make oppositions good at investing substantially in mobilizing poor voters, promising them services, and building grassroots party structures. Without opposition, dominant parties are not pressed to mobilise poor voters or to deliver services (Keefer & Khemani, 2003: 938).

But just how much opposition and contestation produces this pressure for broad-based service delivery? A recent study by Pradeep Chhibber and Irfan Nooruddin of party systems in different Indian states demonstrates that a significant part of the variation in state government expenditure on public goods can be explained by differences in their party systems. Using data over a 30-year period they demonstrate that states with just two-party competition provide more public goods to more people than do states with multi-party competition. In the latter case, because only a simple plurality of votes is needed to win elections, parties use targeted or 'club goods' rather than universally available public goods to mobilise particular, often caste-defined, segments of the population. In two-party contests, there are incentives to make cross-sectional appeals and therefore to provide more widely available public goods (Chhibber & Nooruddin, 2004).

(c) Leadership and political skills. Single-minded leadership can push through reforms in the absence of popular consent let alone elite consensus – this was the case in Britain under Thatcher, Chile under Pinochet, and to some extent Ghana under Rawlings. In each case leaders were able to rely on a secure political position even without a broad mandate, but the conditions for achieving this political security were not only unusual but, in the case of Chile and Ghana, undesirable. While the exercise of 'persistent political will' (March & Olsen, 1989, chapter 2) can serve to bring radical change against tremendous odds, for most leaders it is essential to generate support from

opponents and to cultivate constituencies for reform. According to Guillermo O'Donnell the prisoner's dilemma that confounds efforts to manage economic and political change simultaneously can be overcome by 'finding areas ... in which skilled action (particularly by the government) can lengthen the time horizons (and consequently the scope of solidarities) of crucial actors' (1993: 1376).

Tactics employed by skilled political actors attempting governance reform often require deception – what has become known as 'reform by stealth'. These strategies are intended to 'soften the edge of political conflict by promoting change in the guise of continuity, and to arrange clandestine compensation for groups who perceive reform as a threat' (Jenkins, 1999: 52). Informal and formal institutions that connect public decision-makers to society are crucial for the effectiveness of strategies to drive under-the-table bargains, to divide interests, or to rationalise exemptions for particular groups from painful aspects of reform.

Cohesion within the executive is felt by some observers to explain why seemingly propitious conditions for reform – such as majority governments backed by disciplined parties – are effective in some contexts but not others. Schneider and Heredia (2003), for instance, suggest that the contrast between Brazil and Argentina's reform histories can be explained in part by executive determination. Argentina's disciplined parties and strong governments have failed to prevent reversals in administrative reforms, while party factionalism in Brazil did not prevent recent presidents from enacting administrative reforms. Reforms in Mexico, Thailand, Hungary, and Brazil in an earlier phase were stalled by infighting within the executive branch of government.

Variables Shaping Perceived Risk of Reform

Experiences with governance reform are still so varied and context-contingent that it remains extremely difficult to model reform paths. As Kaufman notes, existing approaches (rational choice models, institutional economics and sociology) do not provide '*ex ante* predictors of reform outcomes', but 'they may provide some insights into the openings and obstacles that potential reformers may face' (2000: 296–297). While there are many factors that influence policy outcomes, we focus here on those that appear most significant, according to a range of recent studies, in bolstering *the capacity of the executive branch to take political risks* in undercutting the privileges of elites accustomed to seeking rents through the state. In other words, they are features of institutions that build trust between state and civil society, improve the 'transmission' of information between state and civil society, and decrease the intransigence of established elites and of civil society groups, enabling new constituencies for reform to be built.

These variables are in essence the features of governance and politics in a particular context that will either entrench patron–client or patrimonial politics, or create the possibility of challenging those politics. They can be divided into structural features of politics and society (longevity of formal institutions, composition of the governing elite, and of civil society), and design features of reform itself (measures to create early wins, to enable reforms to be monitored by the public, etc). They are listed below:

Structural features of politics and society:

(a) *Institutional depth.* The longevity, flexibility, adaptability and legitimacy of major formal and informal institutional channels through which agreements are reached between contending social groups, or through which losers are compensated, enable reformers to generate stronger support for reform and lower the cost of experimentation.
(b) *Composition of governing elites.* Traditional (especially rural landholding) elites can inhibit pro-poor reform efforts. Governing elites relying mainly on clientelist systems for their political power can inhibit the development of effective pro-reform coalitions.
(c) *Composition of civil society.* A diverse civil society with institutions capable of developing horizontal solidarities can provide incentives to reformers by responding positively to reforms and thereby widening reformers' support base.

Design and implementation variables:

(a) *Sequencing, timing and pace of reform.* There is less risk to reformers if reforms generate early 'winners' who can support follow-on reforms, or disarm resistors through a gradualist approach.
(b) *The technical capacity of the public administration.* Public sector capacity constraints blunt the implementation and impact of reforms that are championed by political leaders and command public support.
(c) *Levels of decentralisation.* The devolution of responsibility for some reforms to lower levels of government can deflect some of the opposition to reform, but also encourage experimentation and competition between different levels of government to gain from reform.
(d) *Monitorability* of *reform.* The more open to public scrutiny and measurement, the more likely governments will stick to reform promises.

We address each element in turn.

(a) Institutional Depth: Longevity, Predictability and Legitimacy

Longevity and security of the formal institutional arenas in a country – the political regime, the rules of political competition, and the systems for civilian control over the military – reduce risks and increase willingness to bargain because a sense of institutional permanence extends the time horizon of elites and increases their tolerance of short-term reform costs. This sense of institutional predictability and legitimacy can enable politicians to resist incentives to privilege the short over the long term. Where there is insecurity or where there is a live memory of catastrophic failure in the formal institutional set-up there may be less willingness to take risks. On the other hand, where public institutions have survived threats and crises, there may be a greater willingness to submit to painful reforms. One study of civil service pay reform in eight African countries argues that it is this feature (which the authors simply label 'high institutionalisation') that explains the relative effectiveness of pay reform in Tanzania and Botswana (Kiragu *et al.*, 2004).

Arguably stability of this kind is particularly important for reform prospects in Africa, where the absence of an institutional memory of ousted parties regaining power through peaceful means makes incumbents resist reforms that might undermine patronage power-bases. If the loss of public office is likely to be irrevocable and permanent, there is no incentive to take risks (Allen, 1995: 304).

(b) Composition of Governing Elites

The sustainability of reforms depends on the formation of pro-reform pacts among the major interest groups and actors in a society. For instance, in Japan and other East Asian countries, intimacy between key bureaucracies and the private sector made state and market pull in the same direction to ensure that the combined public–private drive to attain growth was so effective (Wade, 1990). Governing elites are a bureaucratic, political, economic, and often military core policy circle surrounding the chief executive. It should above all exclude traditional proprietary interests (see Sklar, 1987) if it is to avoid cronyism (the Marcos regime in the Philippines), a predatory character (Haiti, Zaire, Uganda under Obote), or the immobilism resulting from change-averse elites as has been the case in India during some periods. We observed earlier that left-of-centre parties have been more effective than others in promoting pro-poor spending, and this is not least because they have been able to circumvent traditional land-owning elites who most directly oppress the rural poor. In Latin America this has been the case wherever effective land reform was pursued (Ascher, 1984). A recent study of the impact of concentrations of traditional land-owning elites in India on the distribution of public goods reinforces the impression that they can constrain pro-poor reform (Bannerjee, 2002). Bannerjee finds that where traditional landlords concentrate land ownership and wealth, and therefore political power, there has been less pressure on the state to deliver public goods of importance to the poor, and a culture of antagonism between peasants and local elites also distorts incentives on decision-makers to take risks in advancing reforms (2002: 5–6).

Another much-observed constraint to risk-taking by executives contemplating administrative reform is a high degree of 'fusion' between political and bureaucratic elites (Schneider & Heredia, 2003: 19) – this inhibits politicians from threatening the securities of bureaucrats in the public administration. As Schneider and Heredia note, because of this, elected officials with weak links to bureaucrats – or political outsiders – will be more open to reform proposals. But paradoxically, without support from bureaucrats, they will be less able actually to implement reforms (Schneider & Heredia: 15). This is part of the complex challenge of maintaining executive and bureaucratic 'autonomy'. Insulation of bureaucrats from politicians and vice versa is seen as an important objective and indeed method of reform, yet examples of effective reform often demonstrate a close relationship between politicians and bureaucrats. For instance, explanations for the successes of the South African Revenue Service, set up as an autonomous executive revenue agency, stress the importance of the ANC's active engagement with the institution, in particular brokering the cooperative relationship between the revenue service and the treasury (Smith, 2003: 7).

The nature of relations with business elites is probably even more important than the capacity of the governing elite to create communication channels with poor groups, as business elites supply the revenues needed for pro-poor spending, and their buy-in is essential (Brautigam, 2004: 12). In Brazil, for instance, modern urban elites tend largely to support the Landless Workers Movement's proposals for land reform, because of an (perhaps mistaken) expectation that land reform would help to clear urban slums (Moore & Putzel, 1999). In Maharashtra, urban professionals have supported the rural Employment Guarantee Scheme by shouldering an extra tax burden for decades, out of a similar expectation that this would contain poverty and its discontents in the countryside (Joshi & Moore, 2000).

An emerging trend supporting reform initiation is the infiltration of policy elites by professionals trained in international financial institutions. According to a recent study by Sengupta, economists once employed by the World Bank entered key economic planning institutions in the Indian central government over the 1980s. Sengupta argues that this cadre of high-level lateral entrants made a significant input to economic reform in the 1990s, using informal levers and networks rather than much-resisted conditionalities to create a persuasive argument for reform and to provide support to reforming politicians (2004). In Argentina and Brazil, 'change teams' advising governments on the design of reform projects likewise have been strongly shaped by international influences in the form of foreign consultants or local advisors closely connected to international financial institutions (Santiso, 2004).

(c) Diversity and Depth of Civil Society: Support for and Monitoring of Reform

Civil society reaction to reforms is an important element of the incentive structure facing reformers. When governing elites take a gamble on reform they often hope that new constituencies will emerge that benefit from and will support reform. They depend on the elasticity of civil society to absorb shocks and re-group around new interests that emerge from reform. Social fragmentation and extremes of inequality can inhibit the ability of citizens to reward development performance in the provision of pubic goods. Ethnic fractionalisation, class conflict, and other sources of social division has been shown to distort the distribution of public goods (Bannerjee, 2002), therefore politicians may not be able to claim credit for reforms of public spending patterns and delivery systems that ought to have remedied distributional problems.

   Civil society institutions can sometimes help interest groups to change their perceptions of their interests and help them to capitalise on new opportunities available through reform. Civil society and the media also play a key role in alerting voters to policy failures, corruption, or the absence of a pro-poor focus in the work of a particular government. Civil society that is 'thin' (i.e. mostly urban-based associations, with no engagement with traditional informal rural institutions) or fearful (wary of repression or co-optation by the state) will be able to do none of these things (Robinson & Friedman, 2007: 661).

(d) Sequencing, Timing, and Pace of Reforms

The sequencing of reform in such a way as to generate early 'winners' from reform, who can then support follow-on reforms, can diffuse resistance. Reform leaders will take decisions on the best sequence of reforms according to their calculations of likely resistance as well as calculations about the pay-offs of reforms in relation to the timing of electoral tests. They may sequence longer-term and more painful reforms (civil service reform) after more visible, popular, and easier to implement ones (decentralisation, performance measures in public services, strengthened public expenditure accountability systems). Or they may envelop reform clusters with economic populism in order to make the entire bundle more palatable and to distract some opponents. These strategies of sequencing and bundling will influence the performance of reforms. Designing reform so that it is barely noticed, is introduced gradually, and that changes institutions over the long run, requires substantial political skill.

(e) Technical Capacity

Public sector reform in industrialised countries over the past 20 years has shown that even where the case for reforms is championed by political leaders, and accepted by society, attitudinal and capacity problems in the administration can blunt the impact of reforms (Caiden, 1991). Capacity problems are acute in low-income crisis-ridden countries, and bureaucrats who lack the infrastructure, training, and commitment to pursue reform will eliminate any positive effects that might emerge from having well-organised constituencies for reform and enthusiastic champions. As noted earlier in this article, the paradox is that complex institutional reforms to improve fiscal stability, managerial efficiency, and political accountability rely for their implementation upon high state capacity – the very quality that is lacking in many developing country administrations (Hutchful, 1999; Mkandawire & Soludo, 1999).

Specialists in public administration argue persuasively that capacity reforms that rest on market models (such as new public management) cannot be pursued where a professional civil service is not fully formed (Nickson, 1999). Flexible and deconcentrated administrative structures, performance measurement systems and the like will not work outside of a shared professional culture and common ethical standards (Bangura, 2000: 43). In other words, as Bangura spells out, 'Only those countries that have established a professional civil service – the foundations of 'old public administration' – may be in a position to move towards 'new public administration' (2000: 43).

Technical capacity has been a particular problem in Africa (Schiavo-Campo *et al.*, 1997) – exacerbated by the decline in funding for higher education (Bangura, 2000: 35). Public sector reform programmes in the 1990s, in recognition of this problem, sought to enhance local ownership through compensatory schemes for top civil servants, training, and equipment supply. Bangura argues that these efforts to rectify the dependency problem in African technical capacity have not achieved much because the continued emphasis on quick results prioritises short-term palliative measures rather than long-term investment in tertiary education and professional public service training (2000: 3). The practical and political problems of improving administrative capacity in low-income states are phenomenal. The costs of pay reform, retrenchment, training, and improving infrastructure are considerable, and frequently contradict reform objectives of reducing the wage share of recurrent expenditure and the overall central government bill as a percentage of GDP per capita (Schiavo-Campo *et al.*, 1997).

A matter of concern in reform processes is the extent to which first-generation reforms and methods to implement them may undermine state capacity to implement second-generation reforms. Carlos Santiso articulates this problem as two important paradoxes of governance reform. First, reforms introduced by decree or by stealth can exacerbate dysfunctions of weak democracies, eroding state legitimacy and credibility, and undermining political skills and capacities to generate supportive coalitions for second-generation reforms. Second, 'shock therapy', dramatic retrenchment programmes and the like, can undermine the capacity of bureaucracies to implement second-generation reforms, considered more demanding of state monitoring and regulatory capacities than earlier adjustment-related reforms (2003). Institutions created *de novo*, set up as autonomous executive agencies, can have the effect of undercutting the state's institutions that would normally be needed for the successful implementation of governance and other development programmes (Wise, 2003: 151). This problem has been examined for Peru by Cecilia Blondet, who argues that efforts to insulate economic policy-making failed simultaneously to strengthen state capacity to implement policy, and in particular neglected institutional development in social sectors. Social sector bureaucracies have in consequence increasingly become arenas for patronage and discretionary action, and their capacity to respond to accountability and efficiency reforms is correspondingly weakened (Blondet, 2004: 6).

(f) Levels of Reform: Devolution to Sub-national Governments

Governance reforms can be pursued at sub-national levels prior to being attempted in central government. When central governments oblige, through the use of conditionalities, federal or lower-level governments to take charge of some painful reforms, this can be an effective means of triggering buy-in to reform, as well as encouraging innovative and locally appropriate strategies. Federal systems may endow sub-national governments with the autonomy to experiment with reforms that can provoke adaptation elsewhere.

There are several reasons why federal systems can offset the risks involved in governance reforms. First, economic or political groups that would be powerful at the national level, acting in concert, may be faced down one at a time, state-by-state. This appears to have been the case in Brazil, where the resistance of provincial governors to fiscal discipline may have been eroded through state-by-state budgetary reforms. Second, pursuit of reforms at sub-national levels can enable policy learning from state to state, and state to centre. Competition between jurisdictions opens space for experimentation with reform, and can help in undermining resistance.

Devolution of responsibility for reform serves many functions – it deflects conflict from the national to a sub-national level, it distributes costs and benefits of reform, it engineers buy-in from doubters not only within the ruling party but amongst opposition parties who may be in charge of sub-national legislatures. It also initiates a race to reform – a phenomenon that has been noted in China and India, where sub-national governments compete with each other in reforming their states in order to attract investment. Thus in China, Montinola *et al.* note that 'federalism, Chinese style', 'provides considerable protection for China's reforms, including limits on the central government' (1995: 52; cited in Jenkins, 1999). This is because political and economic reform has built up the authority of provincial politicians, making it more difficult for the central government to retreat from reform. Decentralisation of reform efforts also creates incentives to experiment and sustain reforms. Experimentation attracts praise and investment, and provokes neighbouring or rival jurisdictions to follow suit. Elites benefiting from reform in one state lose interest in obstructing reform, while those in jurisdictions that have not reformed lose credibility when they oppose reform that has clearly worked well elsewhere in the country (Jenkins, 1999: 71).

More commonly, of course, reforms that rely on the competitive dynamic of devolution and decentralisation face a number of risks owing to capacity constraints. For instance, public management reforms that expand the autonomy of local administrations require good monitoring, inspection and information systems, sound budgetary control, reliable performance indicators and measurements, and a capacity to manage communications and accountability systems between central ministries and a multitude of decentralised agencies (Larbi, 1999; Nickson, 1999). These are precisely the capacities that are very weak at sub-national levels of government in developing countries, and thus decentralised management can exacerbate problems of capture and corruption – as was discovered in Ghana's decentralised management units (Ayee, 1994; Larbi, 1999) and Zimbabwe's regionalised performance management system (Therkildsen, 1999).

The decentralisation of reform efforts can weaken the resolve and command capability of reform-oriented governments if the party system is fragmented and parties are undisciplined. In Brazil, for instance, deputies to the national Congress depend on state-level politicians for support, and will be motivated to vote in ways that support state governments. This means that national government reformers cannot advance reforms in areas that state-level politicians want to resist because they would affect state-level patronage systems. For instance, in order to generate agreement on key economic reforms in the 1990s, the Collor and Cardoso governments were obliged to roll-over billions of dollars in state-level debts, making it impossible for the central government to bring its fiscal accounts into order (Hagopian, 1998: 29).

(g) 'Monitorability' of Reform

The relative 'monitorability' of governance reforms may determine the sustainability of government commitment to them. If reforms can easily be 'tracked' by opposition members of parliament, or by civil society observers, public decision-makers may feel pressure to stick to them rather than allowing them to be undermined by special interests.

Monitorability of reform varies according to types of reform. Accountability reforms such as budget transparency, anti-corruption institutions, and judicial reform may be relatively open to civil society engagement and indeed may even institutionalise a role for civil society participation (for instance through complaints submission procedures).

Monitorability can vary according to the openness with which reforms have been pursued – but this in turn can depend on a government's perception of the support for reform available in civil society or even amongst the opposition. In Brazil, for instance, decision-making processes on reform have been kept open to pressure from organised interests because these are mostly progressive. In contrast, in Madhya Pradesh, the most potent organised interests are reactionary and so reform debates have been kept relatively closed.

Conclusion

Institutions shape incentives to engage in reform, and informal institutions appear decisive in some contexts in determining the prospects of reform. They can ensure that reform is accepted and internalised, or they can subvert reform by reproducing narrow and exclusive access to state resources. The way the connections between state and society enable successful negotiation and internalisation of pacts in favour of reform, and provide for the improved development of external accountability systems, has perhaps not received enough attention in public sector and governance reform programmes. Instead, there can be an emphasis on treating institutions as somewhat self-contained bodies, addressing internal processes and mechanisms rather than the connections between the public sector and society (Carothers, 1999).

Reforms that involve incremental institutional change and do not profoundly modify the elite pacts upon which institutional equilibrium rests are more easily pursued than wholesale institutional change. Examples of the latter are rare, and appear to coincide with major changes in the political landscape, for instance in relationships between the executive and the legislature, or in the nature of party competition.

This article has argued that prospects for governance reforms and the institutional changes they imply will depend on the way politics in any particular context shapes elite investment in clientelist systems, and the way a set of institutional and policy design variables can reduce the perception of the riskiness of reform for politicians keen to stay in power and to take credit for reform. These variables include the domestic institutional inheritance of predictability and legitimacy in formal institutions, the amenability of governing elites to reforms that would oblige them to seek wider support bases, and the capacity of civil society to respond positively to support reforms. Policy design-related variables include the devolution of responsibility for some reforms to lower levels of government, the capacity of the bureaucracy to implement reforms in spite of individual resistance, the sequencing of reforms to generate early successes or to divide and scatter losers from reform, and the extent to which reforms may be monitored by interested parties. It is essential that reform efforts are designed in such a way as to downplay the political threat represented by reform, broker the formation of pro-reform coalitions, cushion the shocks of reforms, or make reform more attractive to voters by delivering tangible benefits.

Notes

1. Bates and Krueger (1993); Harvey and Robinson (1995); Herbst (1993); Nelson (1994); Toye (1992); Jenkins (1999); Birdsall and de la Torre (2001).
2. Diamond and Plattner (1995); Haggard and Kaufman (1995); Dominguez and Shifter (2003).
3. Leftwich (1996), Sklar (1987).
4. Keefer and Khemani (2003); van de Walle (2000).
5. Kidd and Richter (2003).
6. For instance Gould and Ojanen (2003); Booth (2003); Bangura (2000); Schiavo-Campo *et al.* (1997); Nunberg (1989); Larbi (1999).
7. Naim (1995); Pastor and Wise (1994); Geddes (1994); Polidano (2001); Krueger (2000); Schneider and Heredia (2003).
8. There is a growing sense that these two views of governance reform must be reconciled; that reforms to ensure the sound management of economic institutions cannot progress without addressing inequities in the economic system and problems with the legitimacy of the power structure. This is because, for 'economic management' reforms to take effect, issues of equity and legitimacy are central, not least because the ways they are addressed will determine the extent of support these reforms enjoy from a wide range of social groups (Santiso, 2001: 4). Or, to put it another way, the *effectiveness* of the state will be determined in part by the *legitimacy* or credibility of the state and the governing authority.
9. Analysts stressing the role of a renewed public sector ethos include Tendler and Freedheim (1994); Grindle and Hilderbrand (1995); Pratchett and Wingfield (1996).

References

Allen, C. (1995) Understanding African politics, *Review of African Political Economy*, 65, pp. 301–320.

Ascher, W. (1984) *Scheming for the Poor* (Cambridge, MA: Harvard University Press).

Ayee, J. R. A. (1994) Corporate plans and performance contracts as devices for improving the performance of state enterprises, *African Journal of Public Administration and Management*, No. III, pp. 77–91.

Bangura, Y. (2000) *Public Sector Restructuring: The Institutional and Social Effects of Fiscal, Managerial and Capacity-Building Reforms*, UNRISD Occasional Paper No. 3 (Geneva: United Nations Research Institute on Social Development).

Bannerjee, A. V. (2002) *Who is Getting the Public Goods in India: Some Evidence and Some Speculation*, mimeo (Cambridge: Massachusetts Institute of Technology).

Barkan, J. D. (2000) *Increasing Public Sector Accountability and Transparency in Tanzania: An Assessment of the Political Context of Economic Reform*, mimeo (Dar-es-Salaam: World Bank).

Bates, R. H. & Kruger, A. O. (Eds) (1993) *Political and Economic Interactions in Economic Policy Reform* (Oxford: Blackwell).

Birdsall, N. & de la Torre, A. (2001) *Washington Contentious: Economic Policies for Social Equity in Latin America* (Washington DC: Carnegie Endowment for International Peace Press).

Blondet, C. (2004) National machineries for gender equality, Instituto de Estudios Peruanos. Paper presented at the Experts Group meeting on National Women's Machinery, convened by the UN Division for the Advancement of Women, Rome 29 November–2 December, mimeo.

Booth, D. (2003) *Fighting poverty in Africa: Are PRSPs making a difference?* mimeo (London: Overseas Development Institute).

Brautigam, D. (2004) *The People's Budget? Politics, Power, Popular Participation and Pro-Poor Economic Policy*, mimeo (Washington, DC: School of International Service, American University).

Caiden, G. (1991) *Administrative Reform Comes of Age* (New York: De Gruyter).

Caiden, G. (1994) Administrative corruption revisited, *Philippine Journal of Public Administration*, 38(1), pp. 1–16.

Campos, J. E. & Pradhan, S. (2003) A *Framework for Studying Governance Reforms at the Country Level*, mimeo (Washington DC: World Bank).

Carothers, T. (1999) *Aiding Democracy Abroad, The Learning Curve* (Washington DC: Carnegie Endowment for International Peace).

Chhibber, P. & Nooruddin, I. (2004) Do party systems count? The number of parties and government performance in the Indian States, *Comparative Political Studies*, 37(2), pp. 152–187.

Diamond, L. & Plattner, M. (Eds) (1995) *Economic Reform and Democracy* (Baltimore, MD: Johns Hopkins University Press).

Dominguez, J. & Shifter, M. (2003) *Constructing Democratic Governance in Latin America* (Baltimore, MD: Johns Hopkins University Press).

Geddes, B. (1991) A game-theoretic model of reform in Latin American democracies, *American Political Science Review*, 85(2), pp. 371–392.

Geddes, B. (1994) *Politicians' Dilemma: Building State Capacity in Latin America* (Berkeley: University of California Press).

Gould, J. & Ojanen, J. (2003) *Merging in the Circle: The Politics of Tanzania's Poverty Reduction Strategy*, Policy Papers 2/2003 (Helsinki: Institute of Development Studies, University of Helsinki).

Grindle, M. & Hilderbrand, M. (1995) Building sustainable capacity in the public sector: what can be done?, *Public Administration and Development*, 15, pp. 441–463.

Haggard, S. & Kaufman, R. R. (1995) *The Political Economy of Democratic Transitions* (Princeton, NJ: Princeton University Press).

Hagopian, F. (1998) *Negotiating Economic Transitions in Liberalizing Polities: Political Representation and Economic Reform in Latin America*, Working Paper No. 98–5, Weatherhead Center for International Affairs.

Hall, P. & Taylor, R. (1996) Political science and the three new institutionalisms, *Political Studies*, 44, pp. 936–957.

Harvey, C. & Robinson, M. (1995) *The Design of Economic Reforms in the Context of Political Liberalization: The Experience of Mozambique, Senegal and Uganda*, IDS Discussion Paper 353 (Brighton: Institute of Development Studies).

Herbst, J. (1993) *The Politics of Reform in Ghana, 1982–1991* (Berkeley: University of California Press).

Hibou, B. (Ed.) (2004) *Privatizing the State* (London: Hurst & Company).

Hutchful, E. (1999) *From Neo-Liberalism to Neo-Institutionalism: The World Bank, Aid Conditionality, and Public Sector Reform*, mimeo (Geneva: United Nations Research Institute on Social Development).

Jenkins, R. (1999) *Democratic Politics and Economic Reform in India* (Cambridge: Cambridge University Press).

Joshi, A. & Moore, M. P. (2000) Enabling environments: do anti-poverty programmes mobilise the poor?, *Journal of Development Studies*, 37(1), pp. 25–56.

Kaufman, R. (Ed.) (2000) *Sustainable Public Sector Finance in Latin America* (Atlanta: Federal Reserve Bank of Atlanta, Research Department).

Keefer, P. & Khemani, S. (2003) *Democracy, Public Expenditures, and the Poor*, mimeo (Washington DC: Development Research Group, World Bank).

Kidd, J. B. & Richter, F.-J. (2003) *Corruption and Governance in Asia* (London: Palgrave).

Kiragu, K., Mukandala, R. & Morin, D. (2004) Reforming pay policy: techniques, sequencing and politics, in: B. Levy & S. Kpundeh (Eds) *Building State Capacity in Africa: New Approaches and Emerging Lessons* (Washington DC: World Bank).

Krueger, A. O. (Ed.) (2000) *Economic Policy reform: The Second Stage* (Chicago, IL: University of Chicago Press).

Larbi, G. A. (1999) *The New Public Management Approach and Crisis States*, UNRISD Discussion Paper No. 112 (Geneva: United Nations Research Institute on Social Development).

Leftwich, A. (1996) *Democracy and Development: Theory and Practice* (Cambridge: Polity Press).

March, J. G. & Olsen, J. P. (1989) *Rediscovering Institutions: The Organizational Basis of Politics* (Toronto: Free Press).

Mkandawire, T. & Soludo, C. (1999) *Our Future: African Perspectives on Structural Adjustment* (Trendon: Africa World Press).

Montinola, G., Yingyi, Q. & Weingast, B. R. (1995) Federalism, Chinese style: the political basis for economic success in China, *World Politics*, 48(1), pp. 50–81.

Moore, M. & Putzel, J. (1999) *Thinking Strategically about Politics and Poverty*, IDS Working Paper No. 101 (Brighton: Institute of Development Studies, University of Sussex).

Naim, M. (1995) Latin America: the second stage of reform, in: L. Diamond & M. F. Plattner (Eds) *Economic Reform and Democracy* (Baltimore, MD: Johns Hopkins University Press).

Nelson, J. (1993) The politics of economic transformation: is Third World experience relevant in Eastern Europe?, *World Politics*, 45, pp. 434–35.

Nelson, J. (1994) Labor and business roles in dual transitions: building blocks or stumbling blocks?, in: J. Nelson (Ed.) *Intricate Links: Democratization and Market Reforms in Latin America and Eastern Europe* (Washington DC: Overseas Development Council).

Nickson, A. (1999) *Public Sector Management Reform in Latin America*, UNRISD mimeo (Geneva: United Nations Research Institute on Social Development).

Nunberg, B. (1989) *Public Sector Pay and Employment Reform*, World Bank Discussion Paper WDP-68 (Washington DC: World Bank).

O'Donnell, G. (1993) On the State, Democratization and Some Conceptual Problems. *Working Paper 192*, Kellogg Institute, University of Notre Dame, April.

Pastor, M. & Wise, C. (1999) The politics of second generation reform, *Journal of Democracy*, 10(3), pp. 34–48.

Polidano, C. (2001) *Why Civil Service Reforms Fail*, IDPM Public Policy and Management Working Paper No. 16 (Manchester: Institute of Development Policy and Management).

Pratchett, L. & Wingfield, M. (1996) Petty bureaucracy and woolly-minded liberalism? The changing ethos of local government officers, *Public Administration*, 74(4), pp. 639–656.

Robinson, M. & Friedman, S. (2007) Civil society, democratization and foreign aid: civic engagement and public policy in South Africa and Uganda, *Democratization*, 14(4), pp. 643–668.

Santiso, C. (2001) Good governance and aid effectiveness: the World Bank and conditionality, *The Georgetown Public Policy Review*, 7(1), pp. 1–22.

Santiso, C. (2003) *Insulated Economic Policy-Making and Democratic Governance: The Paradox of Second Generation Reforms in Argentina and Brazil*, SAIS Working Paper Series WP/02/03 (Washington DC: School of Advanced International Studies, Johns Hopkins University).

Santiso, C. (2004) Re-forming the state: governance institutions and the credibility of economic policymaking, *International Public Management Journal*, 7(2), pp. 271–298.

Schiavo-Campo, S. de Tommaso, G. & Mukherjee, A. (1997) *Government Employment and Pay: A Global and Regional Perspective*, Policy Research Working Paper WPS 1771 (Washington DC: World Bank).

Schneider, B. R. & Heredia, B. (Eds) (2003) *Reinventing Leviathan: The Politics of Administrative Reform in Developing Countries* (Miami, FL: University of Miami/North-South Press).

Sengupta, M. (2004) The Politics of Market reform in India – the Fragile Basis of Paradigm Shift, unpublished PhD thesis, University of Toronto, Department of Political Science.

Sklar, R. (1987) Developmental democracy, *Comparative Studies in Sociology and History*, 29(4), pp. 686–714.

Smith, L. (2003) The power of politics: the performance of the South Africa Revenue Service and some of its implications, Centre for Policy Studies, *Policy: Issues and Actors*, 16(2), pp. 1–17.

Tendler, J. & Freedheim, S. (1994) Trust in a rent-seeking world: health and government transformed in Northeast Brazil, *World Development*, 22(12), pp. 1771–1791.

Therkildsen, O. (1999) *Efficiency and Accountability: Public Sector Reform in East and Southern Africa*, UNRISD mimeo (Geneva: United Nations Research Institute on Social Development).

Toye, J. (1992) Interest group politics and the implementation of adjustment policies in sub-Saharan Africa, *Journal of International Development*, 4(2), pp. 183–197.

Van de Walle, N. (2000) The impact of multi-party politics in sub-Saharan Africa, paper presented to the Norwegian Association for Development Research – Annual Conference, Bergen, November.

Wade, R. (1990) *Governing the Market* (Princeton, NJ: Princeton University Press).

Weyland, K. (1994) Neo-populism and neo-liberalism in Latin America: unexpected affinities, paper presented at the 90th Annual Meeting of the American Political Science Association, New York, 1–4 September.

Wise, C. (2003) *Reinventing the State: Economic Strategy and Institutional Change in Peru* (Michigan: University of Michigan Press).

Successful Governance Reforms in Two Indian States: Karnataka and Andhra Pradesh

JAMES MANOR

Institute of Commonwealth Studies, University of London

Introduction

This study analyses example from two states, Karnataka and Andhra Pradesh. Two reforms in each state are considered - and in each, one rural initiative and one urban are discussed. In Karnataka, we examine the *Bhoomi* programme, which used information technology to provide farmers with land documents, and the Bangalore Agenda Task Force (BATF), which changed the operations of several municipal agencies. In Andhra Pradesh, we examine the reform of

Metro Water, which oversees that provision of water to the state capital, Hyderabad, and the Development of Women and Children in Rural Areas or 'DWRCA' programme, which sought to provide rural women with credit and thus greater skills, confidence and autonomy.

The first three of these initiatives were substantially successful. The fourth, DWCRA, encountered significant problems, but qualifies as a partial 'success'.

These four initiatives varied in their *breadth* (that is, in the number of sectors or agencies which they affected) and in the *degree of change* that they sought to induce.

Breadth. Only one initiative – the BATF – addressed more than one sector (it engaged with every important municipal service provider in Bangalore). The *Bhoomi* programme was limited to the provision of land documents, the Metro Water scheme tackled only that sector, and DWCRA confined itself mainly to microfinance.

Degree. The BATF sought to induce incremental change within an array of municipal agencies, and yet its impact in several of those was quite substantial. The *Bhoomi* scheme introduced just one change in the means by which land documents were delivered, but this produced significant improvements in a crucial area for farmers. The Metro Water programme proceeded incrementally, but over time generated a thoroughgoing overhaul of that agency's operations. The DWCRA initiative produced changes which in any single village seemed relatively modest and incremental. But it was expanded rapidly and massively, so that it impinged on a vast number of localities.

We also encounter variations in the arenas within which these reforms occurred, and in the groups drawn into negotiations over changes. The BATF and Metro Water programmes entailed extensive negotiations within municipal agencies. But in both cases, consumers and civil society organisations were also drawn into increasingly open policy processes as proactive participants. The BATF made systematic use of civic associations, and brought in external actors and voluntary contributions of funds from the private sector – without resorting to privatisation. The changes made by the *Bhoomi* scheme occurred entirely within one government agency and did not entail an enhanced role either for citizens or for civil society organisations. The DWCRA programme triggered not a change in the operations of bureaucrats but a swift and enormous expansion of existing operations – which placed them under severe strain.

Only one of the initiatives was linked to elected local government institutions. This was the BATF, which engaged with Bangalore's urban council. *Bhoomi*, the other programme in Karnataka, had no connection to the state's strong elected rural councils. This was not a sign of official hesitancy towards those councils. Rather, it was a result of the nature of the programme – it entailed a technical change in the means by which land documents were provided. It is not surprising that the two initiatives in Andhra Pradesh lacked any connection to elected councils at lower levels, since the state government there was more hostile to democratic decentralisation than almost all others in India. The fact that three of the four programmes were not connected to elected local bodies should not be seen as evidence that democratic decentralisation is an unpromising partner for such reforms. It can clearly assist mightily with such initiatives, as it did in the case of the BATF, and as it has done in other Indian states – with for example, the remarkable Education Guarantee Scheme in Madhya Pradesh.

All four of these initiatives qualify as programmes rather than as grand, over-arching macro-systemic policies for reform. They entailed incremental, not radical changes. Both of these things made them comparatively easy to pursue. They involved significant but far from radical changes in political 'pacts' with important interests that provide the underpinnings of the political and policy processes. This does not, however, imply that they deserve a lukewarm welcome. Three of them (the exception being the rapid, massive enlargement of the DWCRA programme) were designed to be practicable amid the political realities that leading politicians faced. They produced patent gains. They were pursued amid a broader array of reforms that offered some promise for macro-systemic change – and enhanced popular faith in the legitimacy of governance reforms.

Three of the four initiatives (the exception being *Bhoomi*) entailed attempts to catalyse participation by ordinary people and demands from them upon governments – even though governments suffered from demand overload. This might seem unwise, but they qualify as 'successes'. How did this happen? There are six strands to the explanation.

1. They enhanced the capacity of formal and informal instruments to deal with demands in a responsive manner.
2. They opened up the political and the policy processes to ordinary people and enabled them to benefit from, but also (to varying degrees) to exert some leverage on those processes.
3. They were also intended to enhance (to varying degrees) the autonomy and capacity of ordinary people and groups.
4. They have therefore tended to be popular with groups that had previously been disaffected or apathetic towards the state administration and the ruling party – so that the popularity of the latter increased.
5. They inspired little serious opposition from important interests.
6. They helped to establish the proposition that well-crafted initiatives – based not just on technocratic principles but on shrewd political calculations – can succeed even when they stimulate greater demand.

The second point above requires more comment. The opening up of policy processes in these has occurred, mainly or entirely, at the 'implementation' stage. In India (unlike Brazil), pro-poor and pro-reform interests are not as yet well organised and formidable. So to open up the process at the design stage is to invite defeat early in the game.

These two states were similar in numerous ways. The administrative machinery available to politicians was quite formidable by the standards of less developed countries. Both had highly competitive multi-party systems (Manor, 1978). Both were witnessing economic booms in major cities but, in each, leaders knew that they had to address resentments among the large rural majority that decides elections. The Chief Ministers of both states (similar to prime ministers in Westminster systems) dominated the making of the policies examined here.

There were, however, important differences. Karnataka had encouraged democratic decentralisation and its bureaucrats saw benefits to them in bottom-up participation, but the Andhra Pradesh government was one of the most hostile in India to the devolution of power (Crook & Manor, 1998; Manor, 2002). The two reforms in the former relied entirely on financial and human resources *internal* to the state, while Andhra Pradesh adapted external models and depended substantially on funds from outside.

Karnataka

The Bangalore Agenda Task Force (BATF)

Between 1994 and 2003, seven key government agencies in Bangalore achieved remarkable increases in public approval ratings for service delivery. Much of the change after 1997, when increases accelerated, occurred as a result of the agencies' interactions with an advisory and oversight body – the Bangalore Agenda Task Force (BATF).

The seven agencies were as follows:

- BMP: Bangalore City Corporation (or *Mahanagara Palike*);
- BESCOM: Karnataka Power Transmission Corporation;
- BMTC: Bangalore Metropolitan Transport Corporation;
- POLICE: Bangalore Police;
- BWSSB: Bangalore Water Supply and Sewerage Board;
- BDA: Bangalore Development Authority.
- BSN: Bangalore Telecom

The increases in citizens' satisfaction are set out in Figure 1.

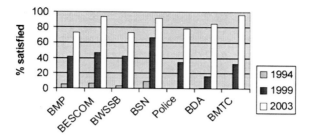

Figure 1. Rise in satsifaction levels
Note: These figures come from stratified random sample surveys conducted by the Public Affairs Centre, Bangalore. They have previously appeared in a World Bank Institute publication

These figures are reinforced by another finding. Respondents were asked whether they paid bribes or 'speed money' to expedite routine transactions with urban agencies. The percentages that had done so were as follows.

1994   20 per cent
1999   23 per cent
2003   11 per cent[1]

Thus, between 1999 and 2003, a marked improvement in service delivery was matched by a dramatic reduction in petty corruption. Taken together, these results add up to a significant 'success'.

The increases in public satisfaction between 1993 and 1999 occurred *before* the BATF was established. They were substantially inspired by the survey or 'Report Card' on municipal agencies' performance by a non-governmental organisation, the Public Affairs Centre, in 1993. The dismal figures in that initial report shocked government services and triggered efforts to improve responsiveness. This ensured that, when the BATF began its work in 1999, it could build on a well-established awareness within government agencies that action to enhance performance was a priority. However, the still more marked increases in satisfaction between 1999 and 2003 – and the decline in petty corruption that had not occurred before 1999 – indicate that the BATF had a significant impact.

Critics note that elected representatives were not appointed to the BATF, and that it reported only to Chief Minister Krishna. Elected members of the City Corporation were invited (along with many others) to attend the twice-yearly public meetings of the BATF, but they were 'largely silent specta-tors'. The critics argue that the BATF was insulated from the political process – elected municipal councillors were not members (Pani, unpub-lished). The link to Krishna placed it squarely within that process, but he saw to it that BATF members were seldom constrained by short-term political concerns.

The BATF's three tasks were to design a process to upgrade the city's infrastructure and systems; to help raise additional resources from citizens; and companies, and to enhance effectiveness and responsiveness of service delivery, build the capacity of service delivery agencies, and suggest best practices from elsewhere (Nilekani, 2003: 2).

Two basic assumptions lay behind the BATF's strategy. First, *government alone cannot meet citizens' aspirations, so problems must be addressed in conjunction with civil society and the private sector*. Second, *existing government institutions have potential* – so *the presumption of state failure should be rejected*.

The BATF did not seek to have the government cede major tasks to the private sector, and it gave only limited emphasis to contracting out to private companies. Instead, it suggested how practices used in the private sector might be internalised by government agencies. BATF members' own funds also covered the cost of the contracting-in of skilled people to provide expertise for a time, free of charge.

The BATF was a public–private partnership, also drawing on civil society. But it was not intended to shrink the state in favour of market forces. Instead, it sought to improve government institutions' performance. At times, it even expanded their roles. The BATF worked *within* existing government agencies – because they were seen to have potential. It rejected the idea that parallel institutions should be created which by-passed those agencies.

Finally, its chairman argued, pragmatically, that constructive change was bound to be incremental and attended by imperfections. It thus developed initiatives that might be sub-optimal, but that would make things better.

The BATF developed two instruments. First, every six months it conducted surveys to gather information on public satisfaction with the seven municipal agencies' performance. Second, an 'accountability platform' was established – public meetings or 'summits' every six months. The media were invited, and most were attended by 700–800 people, including civil society activists. At each 'summit', senior bureaucrats in the seven agencies described their plans for the half-year ahead (providing targets to be met), and reported on work over the preceding six months (to indicate whether earlier targets had been reached) (Nilekani, 2003: 3).

The BATF members had little knowledge of urban governance (Nilekani, 2003: 16) but they offered suggestions for more effective control of agency budgets and initiatives, and more 'customer'-friendly practices. Bureaucrats' interactions with them clearly placed officials under *pressure* to achieve significant change. But several other things provided ample compensation for this. They acquired fresh *ideas* and access to new policy blueprints, to valuable new *resources, human and material*.[2] They gained access to people whose technical skills could help to make new policies work, and to other forms of *financial support*, which some BATF members provided. They felt that they had acquired unprecedented *leverage* over their agencies – thanks to their close ties to the Chief Minister – which might make change possible. And in some cases, they also acquired sufficient *credibility* to attract *further financial resources* – loans from banks and funding from donor agencies.[3]

Their seven agencies retained substantial power and autonomy. The delivery mechanisms almost always remained the agencies themselves. The BATF assisted with initiatives which *the agencies* preferred. Officials were free to reject BATF proposals, and they were often permitted to do so[4] because the Chief Minister and the BATF understood three important things. First, agency officials were far more familiar with the details and complications of implementing changes. Second, officials would be the main bearers of blame or credit for outcomes. Third, allowing them to choose which suggestions to accept would ensure that they had a sense of ownership, which helped to institutionalise change.

Despite its preoccupation with improving service delivery from the *supply* side, the BATF also generated pressure from the *demand* side for better services. The state government gave wide publicity to the improvements achieved. This lifted the morale of public employees, which compensated somewhat for sometimes painful changes in work routines and enhanced their commitment. It also enhanced popular support, while raising expectations, which produced – alongside greater appreciation – greater pressure on agency employees to perform well.

It took time for the suspicions about the BATF among agency officials to wane – as collaborations proved reasonably congenial, and as experiments with new approaches yielded some improvements. It also took time for BATF members to learn how to work with the agencies and what their problems were, and to devise proposals that might address those problems. It thus took roughly 18 months for full-blooded cooperation to develop.

When we consider this alongside the political fortunes of the Chief Minister over the same period, we encounter a significant limitation on the successful working of the BATF initiative. During that first 18 months, the Chief Minister's political stock was very high. But he eventually became embroiled in serious problems. The embarrassing kidnapping of a vastly popular local film star by a forest brigand took months to sort out, an intractable dispute with a neighbouring state over river waters triggered protests against the government, and other problems mounted. These difficulties gradually undermined the Chief Minister's political influence and distracted him (sometimes mightily) from pet projects like the BATF. Much headway was nevertheless made during the four years that this initiative was pursued, but problems such as this – which inevitably arise in democratic polities – need to be considered when we assess efforts at governance reform.

It is impossible here to provide a comprehensive picture of the advances made, but two examples will provide some sense of the trend. First, the Bangalore *Mahanagara Palike* (elected metropolitan council) introduced – at the suggestion of the BATF – a new approach to the collection of property tax, a crucial source of revenue. Property owners were invited to file self-assessments from which their tax obligations were calculated through the use of a simple formula. Payments were then accepted on a 'no questions asked' basis. This liberated taxpayers from the negotiation of bribes to tax inspectors in exchange for allegedly reduced payments. Property tax rates increased a little at the same time, but investigations by journalists indicated that self-assessment still pleased most taxpayers. BATF members estimate that the new system eliminated bribes totalling between Rs100 million and 150 million (between US$ 2.12 million and 3.18 million) *each year*. Revenues soared, which made it possible for the municipal council to undertake numerous development projects.

Second, the financial systems of several city agencies were computerised, and fund-based accounting was introduced – free of charge thanks to funds from a BATF member. Those agencies thus saw things that had been invisible before – empowering them. The number of account heads used by the metropolitan council was reduced from 600 to 30, and it now has – 10 days after the close of each quarter – a full picture of the accounts. This makes it easier to spot leakages and malfeasance, and the new data that it yields trigger action to tackle those things. The new system has worked so effectively that India's Comptroller and Auditor General has used 80 per cent of it in its handbook on best practice.

A state election in 2004 provided a telling popular endorsement of these reforms. The ruling Congress Party lost ground across much of *rural* Karnataka, but in Bangalore – a traditional stronghold of a rival party – the Congress won 11 of 14 seats. The BATF and the achievements of the seven agencies were crucial to that result.

It was not particularly difficult – politically – for Chief Minister Krishna to proceed with this initiative. Other ministers left Bangalore almost entirely to him – because he gave them substantial control over their own ministries. Ruling party legislators were principally concerned with rural constituencies where elections are won and lost. Some became anxious about rural perceptions that the government suffered from urban bias. But Krishna was able to contain this by stressing that the BATF and consequent reforms in the city did not require a significant diversion of resources from the rural sector – and by developing initiatives for rural areas such as the *Bhoomi* project analysed below. Elected urban councillors from his party chafed at first about their relatively limited role, but when opinion surveys were positive, and when many won convincingly in a municipal election, most moderated their complaints.

The main losers in this episode were *low*-level government employees, who had to make painful changes in work routines that entailed the loss of opportunities for self-enrichment. But they had little political influence, they were fragmented within the seven agencies, and the forces that stood above them were too formidable.

The BATF initiative, like the *Bhoomi* project discussed just below, coupled top-down actions and pressure with efforts to catalyse bottom-up demands and awareness. This two-track approach had far more promise than policies that were overwhelmingly driven from above – which had been the norm across India. It was easier to incorporate a bottom-up thrust into these programmes in Karnataka because, since 1983, the main parties had stressed such policies (Manor, 2004b).

The 'Bhoomi' Project

Villagers in Karnataka often make use of an official document called the Record of Rights, Tenancy and Cultivation (RTC) – to show that they own or cultivate a piece of land, to obtain loans and to gain access to certain benefits from the government. It is an exceedingly important document. RTCs have traditionally been issued in hand-written form by village accountants – a system plagued by delays, errors, and demands for bribes. Records maintained by village accountants were closed to scrutiny.

In 1999, the state government began to develop a new system to enable rural dwellers to obtain RTCs quickly and cheaply through computer kiosks in every sub-district headquarters. This was possible because, during the 1990s, the government had made huge headway in computerising land records.[5] With the Chief Minister pressing for action and an effective and technologically sophisticated civil servant in charge, 178 government kiosks were swiftly put in place. By August 2002, the new *Bhoomi* (land) system was operational.

A government employee was available full time at every kiosk to assist those using the system. Villagers had to pay a fee of Rs15 (US$ 0.35) for each RTC. This covered the cost of running the system,[6] and was widely viewed as a reasonable sum. It cost far less than people had paid previously in bribes.

The Chief Minister backed the *Bhoomi* project because it enabled him to counteract two dangerous impressions. The first was the notion that he was too preoccupied with support for information technology (IT) in Bangalore – and that IT held no promise for rural dwellers. The second was the idea that the Chief Minister harboured a strong urban bias. This view was strongly held among member of his own *Vokkaliga* caste cluster, a numerically and economically strong group consisting mainly of cultivators (Manor, 1976). The *Vokkaligas* – whose names often include the word 'Gowda' – have long been suspicious of members of their community who become too urbanised.

Because of his studies at American universities, his caste fellows had long called Krishna 'US Gowda' or (more oddly) 'London Gowda'.

Krishna found enthusiastic support for *Bhoomi* among ministers and legislators in his own party who were anxious about the perceived urban bias. And all bureaucrats except village accountants backed it because they had nothing to lose by it. Village accountants were too dispersed and powerless to resist.

The project worked well as shown by an independent survey of users: 80.3 per cent found the new system 'very simple' to use and 9.6 per cent found it 'simple'; 69.2 per cent of *Bhoomi* users required no help in obtaining their documents – compared with only 25.4 per cent of those using the old method; 42.4 per cent of those using the new system spent 10 minutes or less doing so, and a further 33.9 per cent spent between 11 and 30 minutes. Users of the old system met with far greater delays.

The payment of bribes declined: 97.0 per cent of those using *Bhoomi* kiosks paid none, while 66.1 per cent of those using the old system had to resort to bribes. An estimated Rs 895 million (US$19 million) in illicit payments was saved *each year*. Some 84.8 per cent of those who used the new system rated the behaviour of the staff at kiosks as 'good', while *none* of those who used the manual system took this view (Public Affairs Centre, 2004: 3, 13–18). The overall improvement is clear.

It was also a comparatively easy reform to introduce and to operationalise for two reasons. First – *logistically* – the government possessed or could easily acquire all of the things that were needed to make the project work well. The computerisation of land records meant that required data were already available. Computer networks reaching all sub-districts were largely in place. Computer software to run the system could be speedily developed and tested, thanks to the massive talent available in Bangalore. Computer hardware was readily available for purchase and, thanks to prudent fiscal policies, the state government had the funds available to cover the initial outlay on software and hardware – and the modest fees charged to users would cover costs thereafter.

Second – *politically* – the project had several advantages. This was an incremental change which did not require complex legislation. The Chief Minister threw his weight behind the project, and sustained an intense interest in it until he left office in 2004. The balance of political forces was strongly in favour of the change, and those who benefited vastly outnumbered losers.

Andhra Pradesh

The DWCRA Programme

Andhra Pradesh in the mid-1990s had long lent modest support to a nation-wide scheme for the Development of Women and Children in Rural Areas

(DWCRA). It sought to develop self-help groups among poor women at the grassroots, through micro-finance. After 1996, the state's Chief Minister Chandrababu Naidu pursued it on a far more massive scale after 1996 than anywhere else in India or indeed the world. And this was done with 'governance' clearly in mind. The programme was intended to achieve three main objectives: to change the character of governance processes at the grassroots by drawing huge numbers of rural women into the public sphere for the first time, as purposeful actors; to provide them with financial resources, and to enhance their capacity to manage them productively; and to elicit political support from them for the ruling party.

The Naidu government supported DWCRA and another programme unique to the state – *Janmabhoomi* – despite its hostility to elected local councils (*panchayats*) because it could exercise partisan control over the first two, but not over the councils. But this should not obscure the fact that the DWCRA programme – in part because of its massive size here – had a potent impact on local-level 'governance'.

In 1994, Andhra Pradesh had 10,000 DWCRA groups. In 1997, Naidu decided to establish multiple groups in virtually every village, and pursued this with vigour. Incentives were promised for women who formed DWCRA groups – including subsidised connections to gas canisters, matching grants from the government for their savings, and the possibility of access to loans from a state-generated revolving fund and from state-owned banks.

The Chief Minister had little difficulty in mounting this initiative. He utterly dominated the policy process and state politics. At first, central government funds were available for it but when these dried up the state government used its own resources and then abundant funds from the World Bank's District Poverty Initiative Project.

The benefits that were offered, and the state government's aggressive publicity for them, produced an astonishingly rapid proliferation of DWCRA groups after 1997.[7] There were roughly 370,000 by 2001, 'approximately 400,000' in 2002, and, according to an official estimate, 6.54 million by 2004.[8] Andhra Pradesh (a state with 7.6 per cent of the Indian population) contains over 40 per cent of the DWCRA groups in India, and 20 per cent of all of the women's self-help groups in the world – and most of them had come into being within those seven years. This was both a remarkable achievement and a source of problems.

It was no accident that Chief Minister Naidu sought to make the DWCRA a programme to reach huge numbers of rural women. Two-thirds of voters reside in rural areas, and his much heralded enthusiasm for IT – which many rural dwellers saw as a source of urban bias – posed a potentially political threat to him (as it did in Karnataka). The DWCRA programme was intended to help tackle this.

Women were even more crucial. They had long lent far more support to his Telugu Desam Party that had male voters. But they had done so mainly because Naidu's predecessor, N. T. Rama Rao, had a mass following among women as a result of his vastly popular film career. Naidu had no such link to women voters. He therefore needed to cement their loyalty to his party, and DWCRA became a crucial means of achieving this.

The main impact of the programme has been *psychological* and *social* rather than economic. Reliable analysts of rural Andhra Pradesh comment on the dramatic, widespread change in women's views of themselves. Many have acquired greater confidence and awareness. A smaller number have acquired greater skills, assets, and connections to other women and to officialdom. They have thus become more assertive than their counterparts in most other Indian states.[9] This is no transformation of society, but it is an *exceedingly* significant change.

The DWCRA programme was initially designed for *poor* women, but it appears that large numbers of non-poor women also became involved. This is not surprising – the state government's need to sustain the support of rural women in general drove it to reach beyond just the poor.

The government preferred to foster self-help groups in a manner that would make them beholden to it, so that the ruling party could make its influence penetrate into local arenas. By encouraging the proliferation of DWCRA groups, it was creating new public space within which citizens could participate, contribute their energies to development projects and their own betterment, and make their influence felt. But in so doing, it was also limiting the space for civil society organisations that were autonomous from the government, and crowding the already weak village *panchayats* to the political margins in the villages.[10]

Well-informed analysts in Andhra Pradesh who are sympathetic to the state government believe that the offer of substantial benefits has damaged many DWCRA groups – changing them from self-reliant bodies that gain confidence from their own collective efforts to bodies that mainly access largesse, passively, from above.

Researchers who have done grassroots studies of these groups offer a more complex analysis. They agree that accessing benefits has become the overwhelming preoccupation, and they believe that the resulting passivity has undercut the ability or inclination of borrowers to make productive use of funds. They add that the state government ensured that so much money flowed to many of these groups that they have found it impossible, logistically, to manage the funds adequately.

On the other hand, they believe that, alongside excessive generosity, there existed the *opposite* problem – a failure to provide sufficient, or any, benefits to many of the new groups. Their number is so vast that the authorities found it impossible to deliver on promises to a majority of them.[11] And the push for new groups has caused the abandonment of many older DWCRA groups. As a result, many groups – new and old – felt cheated and angry. Both too much and too little generosity have done damage.

Many older groups which had achieved some viability have been largely abandoned by their members, who join new groups because they believe that this gives them a better chance of accessing benefits. That has wrecked many longstanding groups – and has inspired dismay among women who had begun to flourish within them. And yet many of the new groups have been formed so hastily that they cannot achieve the things (a minimum number of meetings, etc.) that are needed to qualify for benefits from the government – which has inspired dismay among women who switched groups.

Many members of both old and new DWRCA groups were overburdened with other tasks. In some cases, these have empowered group members, but they often compound their problems in managing their resources. Groups were made into implementing agencies in the state government's midday meals scheme for primary schools. They also often played roles in developing nurseries, managing watersheds, building and maintaining minor roads, working with programmes for literacy, family welfare, education and immunisation. The best informed analysts worry that these tasks required women to commit so much time to administration and meetings that they have too little time and energy to tackle their own, already serious problems.[12]

The main beneficiary from their involvement in such work was the government, which badly needed local assistance. At monthly sub-district-level meetings for representatives of DWCRA groups, activists from the ruling party were reported to be present often, 'mostly to organise the release of funds'.[13] This strongly suggests an effort to turn this massive programme to partisan advantage. That conclusion is reinforced by the personalised mailshot communications which many members of DWCRA groups periodically received from the Chief Minister himself. Far from winning their support, this caused many women who feel overburdened and used by the ruling party to direct their resentments against it.

This took its toll at election time. At the 1998 parliamentary election, 45.7 per cent of women had voted for the ruling TDP and its allies, whereas only 36.7 per cent of men did so (Suri, 2002). At the state election in 1999, women had again lent disproportionate support. However, at the 2004 state election, which the TDP lost, women voted *against* it in greater proportion than men[14] – and turned out in greater numbers than men to do so.[15] This was remarkable – the first occasion that women gave it less support than men.

How, amid this litany of troubles, can a 'success' have occurred? There are two things to say here. First, a sizeable number of DWCRA groups have managed to operate in a healthy manner despite these problems. Analysts who work most closely with these groups argue that 85 to 90 per cent of them are in 'dire' difficulty.[16] But that still leaves a significant number – 10 per cent is over 47,000 groups – that continue to function well. In those groups, women have acquired more autonomy in material terms, plus great awareness, confidence and skills – and a willingness to assert themselves more fully in the public sphere.

Second, many of the women in the large majority of DWCRA groups which have run into serious difficulty have been galvanised by their discontents into political action. They reacted against the ruling party in 2004 – a fact that bears witness to the impact of the initiative, even though it was unwelcome to the ruling party – and retain an appetite for self-assertion in the policy and political processes.[17]

Reforming Metro Water – Hyderabad

In the early 1980s, the management of the water supply for the city of Hyderabad[18] was wretchedly managed by an inefficient, unresponsive government agency dominated by engineers. The state government wanted to establish a more dynamic, independent water authority, and it faced 'demands from the World Bank' for such a change. But, until 1989, little changed in practice. In that year, a new agency – Metro Water – was established under World Bank pressure and amid a 'sense of crisis' over rising demand, severe water shortages, and operating deficits (Caseley, 2003: 65–67).[19] The new authority was headed by a formidable civil servant who was not an engineer, and who sought administrative change to enhance service delivery. Its board was chaired by the Chief Minister who gave the new undertaking strong political support, and ensured that it would have greater operational autonomy within the government apparatus. It was restructured to enable consumers to engage with its problems of water supply, sewerage, billing, and pollution control. This enhanced the accountability of the authority, and yielded some gains in cost recovery (Caseley, 2003: 68–75).[20]

During the early 1990s, key posts within it were filled by people skilled in financial management, accounting, personnel matters, and administration. This enabled greater flexibility in the deployment of staff, and a reduction in overtime – which many employees did not welcome – but improved promotion prospects eased resentments. Subsequent improvements in consumers' perceptions of the organisation also eased their anxieties (Caseley, 2003: 75–77).[21]

The reform process was hardly straightforward. Initial steps to streamline approvals for connections to the system reduced delays and many employees' opportunities for self-enrichment. So did action to break a corrupt nexus between employees and private plumbers (Caseley, 2003: 77–78).[22] But this effort was soon abandoned. The most likely explanation for this is that influential politicians were given a 'cut' of illicit profits from the old system.[23] But even these stuttering efforts awakened (mainly middle class) consumers to the possibility of better service. These people were far more self-confident, politically aware, impatient and assertive than the rural women in the DWCRA programme – and they made their discontentment heard more aggressively. Their impact was enhanced by other innovations within Metro Water – for example, new arrangements for official records of customer complaints, and of responses (Caseley, 2003: 78–80).[24]

These things occurred under the Congress Party's government, which was ousted at a state election in 1994. It was succeeded by the Telugu Desam Party, headed from 1995 by Chandrababu Naidu. He pursued reforms with characteristic vigour and attention to detail. He was reinforced by the World Bank – pressure, funding, advice, and arguments that would prove persuasive to the staff. The exercise was largely 'World Bank-driven', but the Chief Minister persisted with it even during a brief moratorium on Bank involvement after India's nuclear tests in May 1998.

Chief Minister Naidu lent strong political backing to senior Metro Water officials who were pressing employees for more comprehensive reform. He also selected extremely able, adroit people for key posts. He welcomed proposals from the Bank for a further streamlining of Metro Water's structures and procedures, the decentralisation of decision-making within it, and measures to check abuses by members of staff. Once again, employees were compensated somewhat by reduced workloads (Caseley, 2003: 80–84).[25]

Central to this effort was a strong preoccupation with the needs and views of consumers. Senior managers were drawn into face-to-face encounters with customers – travelling to locations round the city in a demonstration of outreach. The aims were to make managers more aware of concerns and pressure from citizens, and to bring the latter into the reform process by catalysing participation and demands from them. They responded impressively – and thereafter, Metro Water employees risked 'humiliation' if services remained unresponsive.

Attitudes within the organisation began to change and services improved – thanks to new complaints procedures, the use of data processing to feed complaints into the system, and enhanced transparency and speed of responses (Caseley, 2003: 85–90).[26] The number of customer complaints grew dramatically but satisfaction with the behaviour of the agency's employees *also* increased sharply.

With strong political support, managers then capitalised on these changes by introducing further reforms within the system. Backlogs in connections were tackled through single-window facilities, and by forming teams of the staff members and private contract labourers to provide connections. This inspired some protests from employees, but the agency had been carefully structured to fragment these (Caseley, 2003: 92–105).[27] The reform of Metro Water was patently a 'success'.

The presence of many middle-class customers ensured that reforms received support not just from above, but also from assertive people pressing from below. This was crucial. Such pressure from below is far less easy to muster in reforms that impinge on much less concentrated, less prosperous and less well-organised *rural* populations.

Conclusion

When are governance reforms difficult? There are at least three answers to this question, and they need to be discussed separately.

When they affect the vital interests of powerful groups. The powerful groups in question are politicians at middle or high levels in political systems who possess substantial power; bureaucrats at middle or high levels who possess substantial power; and social groups at any level who possess substantial wealth and (especially) power. To say this is to state the obvious. But what we find to be less obvious is that it is often possible to devise and implement governance reforms that do not damage the interests of these groups, and which nonetheless produce significant improvements in governance for large numbers of people. This was true of all four of the Indian programmes assessed here.

The main losers in three of those episodes (there were no losers except perhaps rural moneylenders in the case of DCWRA) were low-level bureaucrats, but they lacked the power to oppose change. This was true especially because restructuring (in the case of Metro Water) or pre-existing divisions among them (as in the case of the BATF and the *Bhoomi* programme) fragmented them so that they found it difficult to muster collective resistance.

Let us now turn to the second answer to this question: *when certain features of the sector within which a reform is to occur make leaders reluctant to proceed.* Leaders are often reluctant to introduce reforms that render the policy and political processes more open, transparent and downwardly accountable when one of four 'features' is present:

1. When national security issues are perceived to be at stake.
2. When the sector of government that might be opened up is either technologically or technocratically complex, or both – so that senior leaders believe that 'experts' must be left in charge.
3. When the sector yields substantial revenues to the government, which might be lost or reduced if it were opened.
4. When the sector yields substantial profits to private interests and/or senior people in the government – which again might be lost or reduced if it were opened.

The second of these 'features' was present in the sectors affected by Metro Water and some of the initiatives that flowed from the BATF. But in each case, 'experts' remained in charge – indeed, in both cases, greater expertise was imported into the systems. Revenue issues – the third 'feature' listed above – were involved in the cases of Metro Water, the BATF and the *Bhoomi* project. But in every case, the government stood to gain revenues – hardly a disincentive. Those gains occurred in all three cases – especially Metro Water and the BATF – because certain government actors lost opportunities to make illicit profits from bribes. But in every case, those who lost were quite low-level bureaucrats, and their objections could be and were overridden. So in many cases, the four 'features' listed above need not impede governance reforms.

When they threaten serious damage to ruling parties. Indian politicians have tended – in their pursuit of both economic and governance reforms – to concentrate on low-hanging fruit. This has caused many donor representatives and Indian enthusiasts for bolder macro-systemic reform much frustration. But it is important that we look at this from the viewpoint of senior politicians who make nearly all of the crucial decisions in these matters. Two ideas figure prominently in their minds.

First, they fear that if they reach for high-hanging fruit, they risk serious unpopularity and the destabilisation of their governments. An example from the menu of economic reforms will illustrate the point, since similar thinking applies on governance issues. This writer once asked S. M. Krishna (when he was Chief Minister of Karnataka) why he did not consider taxing rural incomes and reductions to the subsidies on electricity. He wearily explained that either action would be tantamount to political suicide. 'They [especially the rural electorate which decides elections] would never forgive me and I would be finished.'[28] A similar response on the electricity issue came from M. Karunanidhi when he was Chief Minister of Tamil Nadu. He told reform-minded advisers who urged him to cut subsidies in that sector that 'if I raise charges on *their* power, they will take away *my* power'.[29] Senior politicians also take this view of audacious governance reforms.

A second idea that looms large in their thinking helps to explain their caution a little further. Once again, an analogy from the sphere of economic reform helps here. An eminent advocate of bold economic reform who holds a senior post in India's central bank recently told this writer that we will never see adventurous reforms in that sector until the country once again faces the kind of economic crisis that arose in 1991. In recent years, despite politicians' hesitancy to undertake difficult economic reforms, inflation has been kept reasonably low, and the economy has grown at an impressive rate. So politicians say to themselves 'since there is no crisis, why take serious risks?'. State-level leaders in India also do not believe that they face a *political* crisis. They concede that fiscal and budgetary constraints make it very difficult for them to maintain their popularity, and that it is exceedingly difficult for them to get re-elected. But in their view, those things add up to a worrying dilemma, not an outright crisis. They therefore prefer to avoid the risks, implied by bolder governance reforms, of high-hanging fruit. They prefer incremental changes, which they develop opportunistically without reference to grand reform models,[30] and which they see (rightly) as practicable. They do not explicitly say that they prefer the practicable good to the risky best which might become the enemy of the good – but that is what is in their minds.

Perhaps we should also see some validity in their tendency to focus on comparatively modest but practicable reforms and, like them, be less preoccupied with macro-level reforms – especially if they pursue change on multiple fronts, as these two state governments did. Perhaps – given the logic of Indian democracy, with its impatient and demanding electorate – this is the best that we are likely to see. This means settling for what Merilee Grindle has called, in a recent World Bank study, the pursuit of 'good enough governance' (Grindle, 2002). Governance in most Indian states is not yet 'good enough' – which justifies donor pressure for change – but perhaps serious multi-faceted efforts to achieve it that have a significant cumulative effect should qualify for at least a hesitant welcome.

Practical Conditions for Successful Governance Reforms

Let us consider what the Indian initiatives tell us about three factors that may influence the capacity of reformers to challenge the privileges of elites and/or to generate support from groups likely to benefit from governance reforms.

Institutional longevity, predictability, and legitimacy

Reform may be difficult where there is a memory of catastrophic institutional failure. This was not a problem in Karnataka and Andhra Pradesh. Institutions there were far from perfect, but they had long been well elaborated, stable, well entrenched – and they had shown some capacity for constructive change. They had never undergone anything approaching 'catastrophic failure'. They had never been involved in the kind of excesses committed by Brazil's military dictatorship – these two state governments spared their people most of the enormities of Indira Gandhi's Emergency between 1975 and 1977 (Manor, 1978). And nothing remotely like the collapse of political institutions that occurred in Uganda before Museveni has happened there.

Even where there was considerable public dissatisfaction with agencies involved in service delivery, considerable 'institutional legitimacy' existed at a deeper level. There was broad popular acceptance of the democratic political system within which such agencies functioned. Indeed, international surveys indicate that such acceptance in India exceeds that found in all other consolidated democracies for which we have evidence – in most cases by a large margin (Linz *et al.*, 2004). In Andhra Pradesh and Karnataka – as in most of southern and western India – that legitimacy had been bolstered by a strong record over many decades in accommodating new actors or entrants within the political system.[31] All of this simplified the task of governance reformers in these two states.

So did the very substantial powers that Chief Ministers enjoy in the Westminster-style systems that exist within Indian states. They have far greater leverage within their political systems than any Brazilian President can hope for – since the latter has to contend with a legislative branch in which no President has commanded a majority of seats, plus powerful Governors in a federal system, some of whom belong to other parties. (Note, however, that President Museveni in Uganda is more powerful than Indian Chief Ministers are.[32]) Since the two Chief Ministers were deeply involved in the four reform initiatives examined here, this mattered.

This leverage was put to good use in negotiations with special interests – another key process noted in our concept paper – that occurred as the BATF and Metro Water reforms proceeded. (Little or no negotiation occurred in the two rural initiatives.[33]) But the main arena for negotiations was not in the huge sphere of state–society relations, but within the confines of state agencies, and the main interests that had to be addressed were the employees of those agencies. Virtually no one within society more broadly suffered pain from the two urban reforms, so no negotiations with discomfited interests there were necessary.

To help drive the reform process forward, both the Metro Water and especially the BATF initiatives drew civil society organisations, organised interests, and individuals who benefited from improved services into the process by using consultative devices. And the BATF also drew in formidable individuals from the private sector.

Changes in composition of governing elites, and the diversity and depth of civil society
The *Bhoomi* programme in Karnataka was implemented by machines and a few technicians who tended them. The other three initiatives drew important new actors into the policy process – with some important differences that need to be discussed.

Only the BATF in Karnataka brought about changes within policy *elites*. It drew in people from the private sector – at the elite level – who assisted urban agencies in envisioning, designing, and implementing reforms. Those people also paid for the services of other technical specialists who assisted the agencies in making these changes. It also systematically included civil society organisations, which helped in shaping some of the changes introduced by municipal agencies, and especially in conveying the views and preferences of citizens to the BATF and those agencies. Finally, the BATF opened up opportunities for ordinary citizens to exercise some voice and influence within the policy process, through publicity campaigns, consumer surveys, and participatory devices.

The two initiatives in Andhra Pradesh did not produce change in the composition of *elites*, but they drew ordinary people into the policy process through the use of participatory mechanisms. The DWCRA scheme differed from the Metro Water programme in that it did not bring civil society organisations into play. We have seen that the Naidu government was suspicious of civil society because it represented independent power centres which it could not control. The DWCRA groups resembled civil society organisations, but they failed to qualify as those because they did not enjoy significant autonomy from the government. Indeed, this was the government's intention. It created such bodies to marginalise genuine civil society organisations. But this still opened up significant opportunities for ordinary people to exercise some influence within the political and policy processes – in the case of DWCRA, previously excluded women.

The Metro Water programme made the governing elite in that sector more diverse. It took an agency that was overwhelmingly dominated by engineers – specialists in the technical aspects of water provision – and brought in specialists in how organisations could be made more flexible, effective, and open. That opening brought individual consumers and organised interests in the urban sector (some of which were civil society organisations) into the margins of the policy process and gave them some influence. They did not become *members* of the governing elite (as occurred in the BATF), but they were linked to it.

Sequencing and intensity of reforms

The architects of the four Indian reform initiatives also paid some attention to the need to take action that would generate early 'winners' who would then support further steps in the reform process – or, where such further steps were unnecessary, the initial changes. There were, however, important differences between the two rural initiatives on the one hand and those in the urban sector on the other.

In the rural sector, the DWCRA scheme in Andhra Pradesh and the *Bhoomi* programme in Karnataka did not entail successive phases of reform. In each case the entire package was unveiled at the outset. Both were pursued in ways that swiftly yielded useful benefits to rural dwellers at an early stage, both to cultivate popular support for the changes and to ensure substantial uptake by villagers.

Sequencing was an important feature of the two urban initiatives. The Metro Water reforms evolved gradually and their character changed somewhat over time as ruling parties and Chief Ministers (with different predilections) succeeded one another. The BATF initiative also evolved gradually – because those involved needed time to consult citizens and numerous municipal agencies over what reforms were desirable and feasible, and because care was taken to draw those agencies into the exercise as willing participants. (Indeed, they had veto power over the potential reforms – and in some cases, they exercised it.) But with both Metro Water and the BATF, some early actions were taken to identify the preferences of ordinary people and to respond to them – in order to generate popular support and pressure for further measures.

This had one further purpose, which is sometimes overlooked in studies of reform. Those early actions were also intended to include many of the government employees whose work practices were changed among the 'winners' from reform. This was done less by offering them material incentives than by two other means. First, many of them gained greater job satisfaction from the improvements in their agencies' capacity to respond effectively to citizens' preferences. Second, they gained greater appreciation and approval from those citizens, which raised their status in the community and their morale. Such things may appear insubstantial alongside the material incentives and disincentives that loom large in many economistic studies of reform. But Tendler's research on Brazil and this writer's interviews with employees in these two agencies indicate that they had a significant impact.

Technical Capacity

By the standards of most less developed countries, state capacity in India is reasonably formidable – and within India, Karnataka and Andhra Pradesh possess it in greater measure than most other states. In particular, both have fairly professional bureaucracies which have not suffered much of the damage that is common in some north Indian states as the result of browbeating by unbridled politicians. The administration in both states is also well de-concentrated, and bureaucrats within it have long experience of working with – and taking instructions from – democratically elected politicians. Corruption among bureaucrats is a significant problem, but it is not as pervasive as in some other Indian states and less developed countries.

The bureaucracies of the two states have their limitations, however. They have often exhibited rigidity, and a reluctance to change. And government employees at lower levels have shown a reluctance to part with some of their former powers as new, more open processes are introduced to permit ordinary folk to exercise some influence. We need to consider (1) how these affected the initiatives assessed here, (2) what politicians, bureaucrats and (in the case of the BATF) others at high levels did to tackle this problem – and (3) how (and how much) pressure from below (from ordinary people who were drawn into the political and policy processes, and from civil society organisations) played a role.

Let us begin with the two initiatives aimed at the rural sector. The *Bhoomi* programme in Karnataka is the most straightforward case, since it entailed a relatively minor change that was well within the capacity of the administration. It was unnecessary to draw civil society organisations into the process, and villagers seeking documents participated as consumers of the service at the same rate as before – but with far greater satisfaction. It was not difficult to force this change upon the village-level officials who were displaced. They were widely dispersed, scarcely organised and thus quite incapable of offering resistance.

The expansion of the DWCRA scheme in Andhra Pradesh required bureaucrats not to *change* their activities but to *expand* them, rapidly and on a massive scale. This placed immense strain on the capacity of the system – indeed the haste with which the initiative was pursued led to its failure in a large majority of cases. Low-level bureaucrats – and ruling party activists who worked closely with them – often concentrated so intensely on increasing the *quantity* of DWCRA groups (in response to heavy pressure from Chief Minister Naidu) that their *quality* usually declined severely. We have seen that the number of such groups was so enormous that even the small minority that worked well provided important new opportunities to the many women who belonged to them but, in general, the initiative was a serious disappointment – to women villagers and ultimately to the Chief Minister who saw rural women turn against him at the 2004 state election. Greater participation from below by women villagers was systematically induced, but this was done in a way that largely excluded civil society organisations from augmenting the technical capacity of the bureaucracy. It is unfair to place most of the blame on the administration. The main problem lay with the unrealistic demands made on it by the Chief Minister. This indicates that reforms should be pursued at a judicious pace – a pace consistent with the capacity of the bureaucracy, which here is reasonably effective – and that the pursuit of spectacular change (with which Naidu had become preoccupied) may well generate more reverses than gains. That should inspire caution regarding the pursuit of high-hanging fruit.

Let us now turn to the urban sector where the initiatives in both states required government employees to make more changes in their work patterns than the two rural programmes did. The reform of Metro Water in the capital of Andhra Pradesh ultimately transformed the delivery of water services. This was only possible because new specialists in organisation and management were drawn into Metro Water, because much more flexible practices were introduced, because the structure was opened to consultations with and pressure from consumers, and because consumers (including, to a modest degree, civil society organisations) engaged with the new process proactively. These were very substantial changes, but their achievement was possible because the time frame involved – extending over the tenure of several Chief Ministers, most of whom lent support to the reform – was far greater than that in which the expansion of DWCRA occurred in the same state. Here – uniquely among these four cases – funds and especially advice from a donor (the World Bank) played a crucial role. That advice helped to ensure that this reform proceeded in a judiciously sequenced way, in a manner that eventually provided Metro Water employees with greater job satisfaction, and at a pace that was realistic given the scale of the task.

The BATF initiative also induced significant changes in the operations of several municipal agencies. This required employees within them to change their work patterns. But the emphasis here was upon augmenting the capacity of those agencies – through the provision of fresh funds, new technologies and methods, technical specialists contracted in, and the opening of the agencies to greater public participation and scrutiny. The media and civil society organisations were systematically included in the policy process, in order to enhance popular participation, accountability and information flows between the agencies and citizens – in both directions. Some of the changes that agency employees had to make placed them under strain. But the much publicised increases in popular appreciation for their services, and the strengthening of their capacity to achieve things, provided them with significant compensation for their discomfort.

Politics and Governance Reforms

A final word is in order here. Some commentators on governance reforms stress the importance of sealing off institutions from the influence of politicians and political crosswinds. The Indian cases indicate that we need to refine this notion. All four 'successes' in India depended on the energetic commitment of the two Chief Ministers, who are of course senior politicians. So the influence of senior politicians did not diminish, it increased – and proved necessary to the successes that were achieved. At the same time, however, one tactic used by those senior leaders was the insulation of institutions that were pursuing reforms from damaging actions by other, lesser politicians who opposed them. But 'insulation' on its own *cannot ensure* the *success* of reforms in an open – and decidedly porous – democratic system such as India's.

These two Chief Ministers sought at least to disarm opponents of the reforms and, wherever possible, to convert them into supporters. They did so by stressing to lesser figures in their own parties (who were, again, politicians) that their futures would be brighter if they cooperated with the reforms – for example, their chances of promotion and re-nomination at the next election would increase. And they persuaded many of those subordinates that the reforms were in their interests – because they were popular and therefore enhanced the re-election prospects of ruling party politicians, and because those lesser figures could claim credit among their constituents for the reforms even if they had not played much part in promoting them. These tactics were at least as important as 'insulation' in turning these initiatives into 'successes'.

The two Chief Ministers also sought to bring new political actors and forces into play, and to use them to construct coalitions to support the reforms. They did so by opening up the policy and political processes (at the implementation stage) to participation by, and to pressures from, ordinary people who benefited from them. They also sought to forge credible commitment mechanisms which could ensure that large constituencies for the reforms would continue to have sufficient voice to make it difficult to abandon changes later. So what was happening was not so much the exclusion of 'politics' and external pressures, but – since it is impossible to exclude 'politics' in such an open system – a change in the political logic, which brought new, pro-reform pressure (from below) to bear upon institutions.

This process of 'opening up' had one other important implication. When senior politicians are crucial to successful reforms – as they were here – there is always a danger that a change of leadership will scuttle them. By opening the processes up, the Chief Ministers (both of whom left office in May 2004) drew enough ordinary people into what is essentially a 'political' game to make it very difficult for subsequent leaders to abandon these reforms. That has not guaranteed their survival – on the contrary – but it has made it politically risky for successors to scrap these programmes. The right kind of 'politics' – more than the exclusion of 'politics' – can contribute to, and not threaten, the sustainability of reforms.

Notes

1. These are again drawn from the Public Affairs Centre survey. See *Development Outreach* (March 2004), p. 12.
2. Nandan Nilekani, who chaired the BATF, provided more than US$1 million of his own money. Others also gave funds generously. Still others gave their time on a *pro bono* basis.
3. Interviews with four of these civil servants, Bangalore, 10–14 May 2004.
4. For example, BATF members tried to persuade the city's transport authority to abandon a destination-oriented approach to its bus lines, in favour of a direction-oriented approach. This would have meant that passengers had to change buses more often than before, but it would have ensured that buses arrived every five minutes or so. This proposal was

rejected, but BATF members were able to assist the transport authority in putting many more buses on the roads – hence the approval in public approval ratings in a sector that mightily affects poor people.

5. Nearly all of the state was covered during the 1990s, and full computerisation had occurred by 2002. This meant that government computers contained – for all 20 million plots of land – information on water rates, revenue assessment, classification of soil, the number of trees, the nature of the possession of the land, partitions of land, mortgages, liabilities, tenancies, crops grown, land utilization, etc. Public Affairs Centre (2004), p. 5. The discussion in this study draws heavily upon this document, which our investigation has shown to be an accurate assessment of the project. The preparation of the Report Card was funded by the Governance Knowledge Sharing Program of the World Bank.

6. In the run-up to the state election of April–May 2004, the fee was slashed to Rs 7, in order to win support from villagers. This fee will mean that the state government will have provided a relatively modest subsidy to sustain the system.

7. Jos Mooij found that estimates of numbers were rather approximate, since it was not always clear whether all self-help groups, or only DWCRA groups, were being counted.

8. Commissioner of Women's Empowerment and Self-Employment (n.d.), p. 1.

9. This comment is based on discussions with APMAS representatives, and more crucially with Benjamin Powis, a doctoral researcher at the Institute of Development Studies, University of Sussex.

10. This view was quite plainly confirmed by two senior strategists from the Telugu Desam Party – interview, Hyderabad, 5 May 2004.

11. For example, DWCRA specialists at APMAS – the organisation that has worked most closely with DWCRA groups – estimates that only 25,000 to 30,000 groups out of a total of around 470,000 have been able to access loans from the government's low-interest revolving fund. The rest are left to seek loans from banks where rates are higher.

12. Commissioner for Women's Empowerment, p. 4, and interview with analysts at APMAS, Hyderabad, 4 May 2004.

13. Interview with analysts at APMAS, Hyderabad, 4 May 2004.

14. The precise figures are, at this writing, disputed. But the fact that a greater proportion of women than men opposed the TDP is clear from the post-poll survey conducted by the most serious analysis of this election. This is the National Election Study, organised out of the Centre for the Study of Developing Societies, Delhi – to whom I am grateful for this information.

15. This was reported on an NDTV election telecast, 11 May 2004.

16. Interview with analysts at APMAS, Hyderabad, 4 May 2004.

17. Some readers may wonder why this analysis did not focus on those other governance 'successes' by Naidu's government in Andhra Pradesh. There are two answers to this question. First, an extremely detailed analysis of most of these alleged successes in 2001 by this writer (an enquiry that was guided by three of the state's most learned and objective analysts) led him to the conclusion that most of the claims concerning these 'successes' were substantially false. (That study resulted in a confidential report to DFID, which was shared with other donor agencies.) Second, in 2004, several of the state's best informed observers of governance programmes (including several civil servants working close to the Chief Minister) advised him (1) that on close examination, other 'successes' would turn out to be major disappointments, and (2) that the DWCRA initiative – despite the ambiguities noted in this text – had accomplished more than those other candidates for inclusion here.

18. Strictly speaking, the metropolitan area served included the twin cities of Hyderabad and Secunderabad, but for simplicity only the former is mentioned in this text.

19. Caseley (2003), pp. 65–67. This entire section on Metro Water draws very heavily from Caseley's study. Field research in the state in May 2004 corroborated his findings in almost every detail.
20. Caseley, pp. 68–75; and interviews with three former executives of Metro Water, Hyderabad, 3 and 5 May 2004.
21. Caseley, pp. 75–77. Interviews with two former employees indicated that, over time, increased customer approval reinforced the head's arguments by yielding greater job satisfaction to members of staff. Interviews, Hyderabad, 6 and 7 May 2004.
22. Caseley, pp. 77–78.
23. Interviews with two former employees, Hyderabad, 4 and 7 May 2004.
24. Caseley (2003), pp. 78–80.
25. Caseley, pp. 80–84. The quotations come from p. 83.
26. Caseley, pp. 85–90. The quotations come from p. 85. Former employees of Metro Water attest to the potent psychological impact of this and other similar changes – interviews, Hyderabad, 4 and 6 May 2004.
27. Caseley, pp. 92–105; and interviews with former managers and employees of Metro Water, Hyderabad, 4, 6 and 7 May 2004.
28. Interview, Bangalore, 7 December 2000.
29. I am grateful to R. Venkitaramanan, one of those advisers (and the former Governor of the Reserve Bank of India) for this information.
30. I am grateful to Vikram Menon of the World Bank for this formulation.
31. See in this connection, Reddy and Haragopal (1988).
32. This is vividly apparent from a forthcoming Machiavellian study of these three countries. See Manor *et al.* (forthcoming 2007)
33. The *Bhoomi* scheme in Karnataka required a sufficiently modest change – from human beings to machines – and the registrars who were displaced were so widely scattered at the village level that this change was simply forced through. In Andhra Pradesh, the Chief Minister tended – far more strongly than his counterparts in Karnataka over the last three decades – to proceed by assertion rather than by negotiation, and that is how the immense, rapid expansion of DWCRA occurred. But the complexity of the changes in administrative practice that were needed within Metro Water forced the government into negotiations.

References

Caseley, J. (2003) Bringing Citizens Back In: Public Sector Reform, Service Delivery Performance, and Accountability in an Indian State, unpublished DPhil Thesis, Institute of Development Studies, University of Sussex.
Commissioner of Women's Empowerment and Self-Employment (undated) Note on Self Help Groups in Andhra Pradesh, Hyderabad.
Crook, R. & Manor, J. (1998) *Democracy and Decentralization in South Asia and West Africa: Participation, Accountability and Performance* (Cambridge: Cambridge University Press).
Grindle, M. (2002) *Good Enough Governance: Poverty Reduction and Reform in Developing Countries*, Prepared for the Poverty Reduction Group (Washington: World Bank).
Linz, J., Stepan, A. & Yadav, Y. (2004) Nation State or State Nation? Comparative Reflections in Indian Democracy. Paper presented at a NETSAPPE conference on Indian politics, Paris, June.
Manor, J. (1976) The evolution of political arenas and units of social organisation: the Lingayats and Vokkaligas of Mysore, in: M. N. Srinivas (Ed.) *Dimensions of Social Change in India* (Delhi: Allied).

Manor, J. (1978) Where Congress survived: five states in the Indian General Election of 1977, *Asian Survey*, August.

Manor, J. (1988) Karnataka, in: M. S. A. Rao & F. Frankel (Eds) *Dominance and State Power in Modern India*, Vol. 1 (Oxford University Press: Delhi).

Manor, J. (1998) Karnataka, in: M. S. A. Rao & F. Frankel (Eds) *Dominance and State Power in Modern India*, Vol. 1 (Delhi: Oxford University Press).

Manor, J. (2002) Democratic decentralisation in two Indian States: past and present, *Indian Journal of Political Science*, pp. 51–72 (Charan Singh University, Meerut).

Manor, J. (2004a) Democratization with inclusion: political reforms and people's empowerment at the grassroots, *Journal of Human Development*, March, pp. 5–29.

Manor, J. (2004b) Explaining political trajectories in Andhra Pradesh and Karnataka' in: R. Jenkins (Ed.) *Regional Reflections: Comparing Politics across India's States* (Delhi: Oxford University Press).

Manor, J. (2004c) The Presidency, in: D. Kapur & P. B. Mehta (Eds) *Public Institutions in India: Performance and Design* (Delhi: Oxford University Press).

Manor, J., Marcus Melo & Ng'ethe, N. (forthcoming 2007) *Against the Odds: Politicians, Institutions and the Struggle against Poverty* (Ithaca and London: Cornell University Press).

Nilekani, N. M. (2003) *BATF: A Partnership with Promise?* (Bangalore: Public Affairs Centre).

Pani, N. (undated) Icons and reform politics: the case of S. M. Krishna, unpublished manuscript.

Public Affairs Centre (2004) *A Report Card on Bhoomi Kiosks: A User Assessment of the Computerised Land Records System in Karnataka* (Bangalore: Public Affairs Centre).

Reddy, Ram & Haragopal, G. (1998) Andhra Pradesh, in: M. S. A. Rao & F. Frankel (Eds) *Dominance and State Power in Modern India*, Vol. 1 (Delhi: Oxford University Press).

Suri, K. C. (2002) *Democratic Process and Electoral Politics in Andhra Pradesh, India*, ODI Working Paper 180 (London: Overseas Development Institute).

World Bank (2004, March) *Development Outreach* (Washington, DC: World Bank).

The Political Economy of Governance Reforms in Uganda

MARK ROBINSON

Governance and Conflict, UK Department for International Development

Introduction

Uganda is widely acclaimed as an African success on account of achievements in macro-economic reforms, poverty reduction, and political stability, following years of civil war, economic decline, and worsening poverty. Progress on these fronts was accompanied by a succession of governance reforms, ranging from an ambitious programme of civil service restructuring, the creation of a series of semi-autonomous public agencies, reforms in public expenditure management, decentralisation, and innovations in service delivery, through to legal and institutional measures to combat corruption.

Despite variations in form and content, success in the implementation of governance reforms in Uganda is often viewed as a function of political commitment, technocratic insulation, and organisational autonomy. The personal commitment of President Yoweri Museveni to improving governance facilitated the introduction of reform initiatives; responsibility for designing the reforms was vested in the hands of a small technocratic elite in key government departments, while autonomy was entrusted to arms-length agencies and secretariats responsible for implementation. These mirror the institutional ingredients that account for the successful implementation of the economic reform agenda, centring on the Ministry of Finance, Planning and Economic Development (MOFPED), with strong presidential backing and high levels of capacity and insulation (Harvey & Robinson, 1995).

These institutional characteristics are commonly thought to explain the early success of governance reforms in the 1990s. But the technocratic assumptions underlying this interpretation are inadequate in explaining the subsequent slowing of reform momentum and the difficulty in sustaining positive outcomes. Uganda's trajectory of early success followed by steady decline cannot be explained by the design of formal institutions without reference to the underlying pattern of politics and informal institutional arrangements reflected in the changing character of the political regime, the influence of neo-patrimonialism, and the nature of incentives for reform. The absence of durable connections between the state and society in the form of active political parties and an engaged civil society may be a factor in explaining both the initial success of the reforms and their failure to take root and persevere (Goetz, this issue).

The governance reforms examined in this article were designed to promote structural changes in state institutions and change the incentives that shape the behaviour of state actors in order to improve the quantity and quality of public goods and services (Campos & Pradhan, 2005). These include civil service reform, reforms in tax administration, the establishment of anti-corruption agencies, and are among the most significant areas of governance reform in Uganda.

Success is understood here in terms of achieving and sustaining the objectives of governance reforms, whether through building administrative capacity, improving managerial efficiency, or strengthening public accountability. Successful outcomes cannot easily be captured by robust macro-level indicators of effectiveness, accountability and probity, and it is difficult to gather clear and unambiguous evidence of impact. It is possible, however, to distinguish between reforms that result in the creation, abolition, or restructuring of formal institutions (such as an independent tax authority and anti-corruption agencies, the closure of parastatal agencies, and mergers of line ministries), and the more immediate outputs of governance reforms, using indicators such as improvements in tax revenues, number of indictments and prosecutions of civil servants, and the size and cost of the civil service establishment.

While the main focus is on domestic political factors, a discussion of governance reforms in Uganda would not be complete without reference to the considerable influence exerted by foreign aid donors. Foreign aid accounts for 52 per cent of the government's budget, and all three reform initiatives under review received significant infusions of donor assistance. Policy initiatives are usually instigated with the technical and financial support of donors, who exert considerable influence over the content and speed of reform. Early success is strongly associated with the depth and persistence of donor support. The sustained support of foreign aid donors also finds reflection in the political domain, with the majority evincing strong and consistent diplomatic support for President Museveni, but with increasing reservations over the pace and depth of political reform.

Politics and Governance Reforms in the 1990s

The National Resistance Movement (NRM) constructed a broad-based alliance after attaining power through successful armed rebellion in January 1986. The government brought together representatives from different political parties and members of different ethnic and religious groups in an effort to overcome the historic divisions that served as the root cause of endemic conflict. Political parties were constrained from operating freely in the no-party system of Movement politics on the grounds that they had contributed to ethnic conflict and civil war under previous governments. The constitution was created through an extended process of consultation that lasted over two years, and was formally endorsed in 1995 by an elected national assembly. Electoral competition was permitted in the Movement system with candidates standing as individuals rather than as representatives of political parties while decentralisation provided opportunities for contestation at lower levels of the political system.

Despite ostensible commitment to democratic politics, the Movement did not retain its broad-based and inclusive character. Over time, the Movement gradually consolidated its power around a group of former resistance army officers with personal, ideological, or family ties to President Museveni. The political base of the NRM narrowed as key members of the government resigned in protest over the increasingly personalised style of politics and flagrant corruption in ruling circles. Ugandans with strong kinship roots in the west of the country accounted for a disproportionate share of top political and military positions and civil service appointments. Having come to power with the intention of eliminating ethnic and religious considerations from political life, kinship, family, and regional affiliations increasingly predominated over the ideological posture that motivated the Movement at its inception. These features of the contemporary Ugandan political landscape, combining personalised rule, patronage, and clientelism, increasingly resemble those associated with the neo-patrimonial politics common in other African states (Hickey, 2003: 32–37).[1]

Tendencies towards the re-emergence of patrimonial politics as the Movement's support base contracted were accompanied by growing demands for the restoration of multi-party democracy, both from the opposition and from reformists within the Movement. A national referendum held on the question of multi-party democracy in July 2005 produced a strong majority in favour of political competition, with the President accepting the verdict. Prior to the referendum, the Ugandan Parliament approved the lifting of presidential term limits, allowing President Museveni to run successfully as a candidate in the 2005 elections.

Despite controls on political party activity, governance reform featured as a major element in the Movement's Ten-Point Programme developed during the struggle against the Obote II regime. In particular, the programme singled out the elimination of corruption, the decentralisation of power, and democracy as key objectives for a future government. While other aspects of the programme relating to the management of the economy were watered down or abandoned following the decision to opt for wholesale economic liberalisation from the late 1980s, governance reform remained a high priority on President Museveni's political agenda.

Political commitment to reform was evident in the early move towards decentralisation from the late 1980s, when the resistance councils created in the areas under the liberation forces became the cornerstone for the five-tier system of local councils. These were established from village to district level on the basis of an elaborate system of direct and indirect elections, and received an increasingly significant share of the national budget (Francis & James, 2003). Government spending on primary health and education is routed through district governments, which have taken on the responsibility for recruiting and paying the salaries of medical staff and teachers. One-third of the budget is now administered by district administration, leading some to observe that the system confers developmental benefits while advancing the Movement's political project (Kjaer, 2004).

Another important area of governance reform is public expenditure management, in which a series of institutional arrangements have been put in place by MOFPED with donor support to manage the budget process and monitor public spending commitments. These centre on the Medium-Term Expenditure Framework (MTEF), designed to maintain public expenditure within manageable and predictable targets, and the government's Poverty Eradication Action Programme (PEAP), which sets out the government's expenditure priorities for poverty reduction and public services.

Three governance reforms are singled out for particular attention in this article: the restructuring of public administration, the creation of the

Uganda Revenue Authority (URA), and a range of anti-corruption initiatives. In each case there is well over a decade of experience of implementation from which lessons can be derived. These reforms also offer insights into different institutional arrangements for governance reform, including structural reforms in public administration, the creation of a semi-autonomous agency for tax collection, and institutional and legal measures to combat corruption.[2]

Civil Service Reform: The Politics of Bureaucratic Restructuring

Reform Context

Uganda's civil service in 1986 was bloated, highly corrupt and inefficient. It was incapable of performing basic service delivery or policy implementation functions. Many civil servants did not turn up for work as rates of pay were nominal and most had other sources of income to meet basic needs. There were a large number of 'ghost workers' on the government payroll who were either deceased or did not exist. Bribery was rampant. The parlous state of the civil service was the product of years of political strife and economic chaos (Langseth, 1995).

As a result, civil service reform is one of the most pressing challenges facing the NRM government. The Civil Service Reform Programme (CSRP) began soon after it came to power in 1986 and has continued under various guises to the present. Its overall goals were to improve the efficiency, accountability, and performance of the public service through a series of reforms. The most radical initiatives were implemented in the late 1980s and early 1990s with an emphasis on cutting costs through downsizing and rationalising the bureaucracy. This was accompanied by the monetisation of benefits and improving incentives through pay reform, along with measures to improve efficiency through functional reviews and ministerial mergers. In the latest phase of reform, the emphasis has shifted to enhancing performance through results-oriented management and the consolidation of pay and pension reforms.

Implementation of the reform agenda began with the merger of the Ministries of Finance and Planning and Economic Development followed by a reduction in the number of ministries through a series of mergers and closures. A radical downsizing plan was prepared with the objective of reducing the total public service to 150,000 by 1995 (Langseth, 1995). These measures were accompanied by large-scale military demobilisation. Non-salary benefits for most civil servants in the form of vehicles and housing were monetised. There was a series of across-the-board salary enhancements in the early 1990s, followed by selective increases for particular categories of staff thereafter with the intention of achieving the objective of a minimum living wage by 1996 (Kiragu & Mukandala, 2005: 257–264). Substantial donor funding was provided for technical assistance and voluntary severance packages for civil servants and soldiers. From the mid-1990s, policy attention focused principally on pay reform with the ultimate goal of paying public servants living wages.

What distinguished the Ugandan programme from similar initiatives in other parts of Africa was political commitment at the highest level. This commitment was evident in the creation of the presidential commission to investigate the reforms, followed by a period of extensive deliberation before the reform programme was officially launched. The decision to initiate the reforms was the product of a careful political calculus in which the potential efficiency gains were balanced against the risk of potential opposition from vested interests within the civil service. President Museveni was strongly supportive of a reform agenda for both technical and political reasons: the pressing need to rebuild the state apparatus in pursuit of the NRM's political project, and to weed out civil servants appointed under the Amin and Obote regimes who could serve as a potent source of opposition to reform.

Impact of the Reforms

Uganda's Civil Service Reform Programme in the 1990s is widely regarded as among the most successful in sub-Saharan Africa. The government succeeded in halving the public service sector workforce between 1992 and 1995. The size of the military was reduced from 90,000 to 50,000. The number of ministries was almost halved from 38 to 21. There was some progress in pay reform with three successive salary increases in the early 1990s (Kiragu & Mukandala, 2005: 266).

However, despite early successes, particularly in reducing the size of the civil service, the momentum of the reform process slowed from the mid-1990s, and the results in terms of pay reforms and efficiency gains were much less impressive. The presidential commission's target of achieving a minimum living wage for civil servants by 1996 was not achieved and public sector salaries remain well below those in the private sector despite successive salary increases. These differentials are even higher for specialised technical and professional cadres such as accountants, lawyers, and doctors, and contribute to growing problems of recruitment (Kiragu & Mukandala, 2005: 281).

The government opted to make selective increases for specific categories of staff, stating that its priority was the recruitment of teachers and health workers to fulfil service delivery targets rather than the pay and conditions of the civil service as a whole. Threatened strike action by lecturers and doctors prompted the government to award them significant increases. Members of Parliament (MPs) and ministers, whose salaries were de-linked from civil service pay scales, also received hefty increases. Public servants with political influence – such as top civil servants, judges, and officials in charge of special commissions and semi-autonomous agencies – also received large increases. Lower grades of the civil service were also granted pay increases from the late 1990s. But the salaries of middle-ranking civil servants in the technical and professional grades increased least over this period.

Another indication of the slowing momentum of reform is the growth in the overall number of public servants, militating against the scope for further pay increases. The civil service had increased to around 218,000 in 2004, mostly on account of large-scale recruitment of teachers.

But there was also marked growth in the 1990s in what can be termed the political bureaucracy, contributing to a steady increase in the civil service wage bill. There has been an increase in the numbers of officials and advisers, central government ministers, and district resident commissioners, performing political and administrative functions. There was also a considerable increase in the number of presidential advisers, autonomous and semi-autonomous agencies, secretariats and commissions, headed by senior-level appointees, all with a retinue of support staff. Finally, the number of diplomatic missions has also grown. The political establishment has also expanded, through increases in the number of ministers, MPs, and districts.

This growth has had a significant budgetary impact, with public administration accounting for an increasing share of government expenditure. However, despite the establishment of a presidential committee in 2002, intended to identify possible savings, the bureaucracy continues to expand.

The slowing down of progress in pay reforms and the untrammelled growth in the political bureaucracy since the late 1990s is the culmination of a deliberate political strategy. Many of the appointees to statutory and ad hoc commissions and autonomous agencies are known supporters of the Movement with strong kinship ties to the President's family, and were placed in positions of authority with approval at the highest level. Such positions can thus be considered as sinecures for loyal followers, as a form of patronage dispensed in return for political support. The political imperative of retaining power through patronage drives the formation of new institutions and new positions in government. This serves to explain the creation of new ministerial posts to reward supporters as the political base of the Movement narrows. It also drives the trend towards political interference in recruitment in semi-autonomous agencies.

Political enthusiasm for civil service reform has diminished considerably since the late 1990s. There is a marked contrast between active presidential engagement in the reform process in the 1990s and the current situation in which the President is openly critical of the civil service. Another factor shaping reform outcomes is the relative weight and influence of different ministries and agencies in the civil service reform process. The Ministry of Public

Service (MPS) plays a secondary role to MOFPED, which is very much the driving force in the reform process from the point of view of budgetary considerations. The Administrative Reforms Secretariat (ARS) is formally responsible for implementing the recommendations of the presidential commission, but now has little influence in shaping the content and sustaining the momentum of the reforms and is politically marginalised.

Outcomes

Civil service reform initiatives registered a significant level of success in the mid-1990s. These had strong presidential backing and produced visible results in the form of sharp reductions in the civil service payroll, improved salaries, and ministerial restructuring. But, for several reasons, it has proved difficult to sustain the momentum of the reforms. Political attention has focused on other, more pressing, concerns. Presidential enthusiasm has waned, reflected in the limited progress towards the minimum living wage and in public statements denigrating the bureaucracy. Lack of visible and sustained progress in education and health delivery has further weakened presidential commitment.

The responsibility for implementing the CSRP was granted to the ARS as a semi-autonomous agency with some degree of operational independence from its parent ministry. But in practice MOFPED exercises considerable influence over reform implementation and budgetary resources. Organisational autonomy is undermined by financial dependence and the lack of visibility at the political level. Not only has the momentum of reform slowed but political compulsions have undermined some of the early achievements. In particular, the increasing share of government expenditure allocated to public administration reflects growth in the political bureaucracy. This contradicts the government's policy objective of maintaining civil service budget outlays at current levels in real terms, and undermines the scope for increasing civil service pay in line with the minimum living wage.

Failure to make progress on pay reform for the vast majority of civil servants contributes to declining motivation. Large differentials between administrative grades and top civil servants, together with special treatment for senior officials in the political bureaucracy and semi-autonomous bodies like the URA, fuel resentment, undermine morale, and provide a stimulus to corruption. The lack of incentives for public servants who have to cope with successive reform and future uncertainty runs counter to a key objective of the reform programme, namely the creation of a committed, responsible, and results-oriented civil service. The failure to adequately incentivise the public service could hinder reform implementation across a range of government programmes and is at odds with many of its wider development objectives. But the political commitment required to fulfil the original objectives of the CSRP is very much in abeyance in the face of political compulsions with institutional manifestations that run counter to and ultimately undermine these objectives.

The Uganda Revenue Authority: The Politics of Institutional Autonomy

Tax revenues were extremely low when the NRM came to power in 1986, estimated at around 2 per cent of GDP. This was the cumulative result of several factors: economic crisis, low rates of private investment, and endemic levels of corruption and inefficiency in the civil service. The Uganda Revenue Authority was established in 1991 as a semi-autonomous agency to improve the efficiency of tax collection and thereby increase government revenue, which would in turn help to reduce dependence on foreign aid. A further objective was, through improved incentives and administration, to reduce systemic corruption resulting from collusion between taxpayers and government tax collectors.

The creation of the URA was a governance reform in which a new institution was created to carry out a set of core functions critical to state capacity. The URA case offers insights into the political determinants of institutional design and performance, demonstrating how autonomy can contribute to short-run success in terms of revenue growth but also foster vulnerability to political influence. This in turn undermines the effectiveness and sustainability of the reform process by encouraging corruption and predatory behaviour.

The URA took over responsibility for tax collection from the finance ministry, which had previously hosted various revenue departments. It brought together these various units under a single agency, providing an opportunity for greater organisational coherence and efficiency gains. The URA was granted operational autonomy for day-to-day affairs in return for agreed revenue targets set by the ministry, underpinned by an expectation that increased autonomy would reduce the scope for political interference (Therkildsen, 2004). Its semi-autonomous status meant that it was exempt from civil service rules concerning recruitment, retention, pay, and conditions, allowing it to recruit internationally at competitive market rates. Two of the first three Commissioners General (CGs) were expatriates, which was defended by the government on the grounds that a foreigner would be relatively inured to political pressure and patronage.

Ministry staffing levels for revenue administration in 1991 numbered around 1700. External consultants recommended a 20 per cent reduction in staffing and retrenchment for low-grade staff and proposed that all those above a certain level of seniority would be re-hired by URA on the basis of re-application and interviews. Most of these recommendations were not implemented, with the result that the majority of recruits to the new authority (with the exception of a number of senior appointments) were former civil servants from the Ministry of Finance. Existing staff were transferred to the URA on probation with a subsequent screening process that produced several hundred redundancies.

Salaries were radically enhanced to provide an incentives regime that would be conducive to productivity and curb rent-seeking behaviour. Aid donors provided salary top-ups that were permissible under the semi-autonomous status of the URA. In 1993, URA staff salaries were reported to be between eight and nine times higher than for other civil servants with scope for payment of a performance-related bonus, though they were no longer eligible for the state pension scheme and lost other civil service benefits. De-linking the URA from civil service pay and the desire to recruit highly motivated professional senior managers were reflected in significant differentials between the top and bottom grades (Fjeldstad *et al.*, 2003: 25; Therkildsen, 2004: 9).

Despite the uncertainty of tenure on account of their contract status the URA was a very attractive place for former civil servants to be located on account of vastly superior pay and conditions, especially for senior staff who were remunerated at levels comparable to the private sector. While creating strong incentives for senior managers, disparities on this scale were a cause of discontent at lower levels and a factor in the subsequent growth of corruption in the organisation. They also provoked resentment from MOFPED officials who received inferior pay and conditions, especially those who were not hired by the URA, some of whom have since risen to positions of seniority in the ministry.

By 2000, the differential with civil service salaries had narrowed to 4–5 times on account of inflation, with a further reduction since then (Fjeldstad *et al.*, 2003: 25). Graduate entry-level salaries are now comparable with other semi-autonomous authorities and it is only at the top level that significant disparities remain. Steady erosion of remuneration is perceived by some to reflect a deliberate policy on the part of MOFPED, provoked by resentment of the special status accorded to URA staff. There is also a perception that URA salaries should not increase further until the rest of the civil service has achieved a living wage. Whatever the cause of diminishing differentials, this aspect of autonomy has become less significant over time as pay and conditions move more closely in line with civil service norms.

Commensurate with its semi-autonomous status, a relatively independent board of directors was established, chaired by the CG, with representation from top officials from MOFPED and the Governor of the Bank of Uganda. It was charged with formulating and implementing policy for the URA and for ensuring compliance with MOFPED directives. These conflicting responsibilities gave rise to a situation in which the Board became actively involved in operational concerns of a more routine nature. A legislative amendment to the URA statute in 1997 sought to redress this problem by changing the role of the Board from an emphasis on policy direction to monitoring revenue performance, recruitment, and procurement. Despite these provisions, the Board remains actively involved in day-to-day operational issues, including decisions relating to appointments. MOFPED exercises a dominant role in Board affairs and supervises the CG, at times making policy decisions concerning tax administration with little consultation (Fjeldstad *et al.*, 2003; Therkildsen, 2004). These changes had important implications for the autonomy of the URA and ultimately for organisational performance.

The initial impact of the creation of the URA on levels of tax collection was impressive. While revenues had already increased from a low base of 2 per cent of GDP in 1986 to 7 per cent by the year of the URA's inception in 1991, these grew to a peak of 12.3 per cent by 1996 (Fjeldstad *et al.*, 2003: 9). The subsequent tax-to-GDP ratio hovered around the 12 per cent level in the late 1990s with no further growth forecast, which places it well below the performance of tax authorities elsewhere in Africa (Devas *et al.*, 2001; Therkildsen, 2004: 6). Despite its early success, the URA has often failed to meet annual revenue targets set by MOFPED. The slowing of revenue growth is partly explained by the erosion of institutional autonomy on account of political interference and deficiencies in the URA's governance and management structures. This was most strikingly evident in politically motivated appointments and transfers that contributed to the resurfacing of corruption and organisational inefficiency (Therkildsen, 2004: 2).

One of the expected benefits resulting from URA's semi-autonomous status was insulation from political interests. Hiving off responsibility for tax administration from the parent ministry was seen as a device to limit politicians' direct involvement in tax affairs, as well as limiting their means of seeking preferential treatment for clients (family and kin members, friends, and supporters) in tax assessment and payment and their ability to exert influence over appointments. However, subsequent experience attests to systematic political involvement in URA affairs, especially through influence over the recruitment, promotion, and transfer of staff. Ministers, family members with political connections, and political advisers in State House have all sought to exert influence in this manner.[3] Many of these appointments were individuals from the west of the country, provoking allegations of ethnic bias. Recruitment procedures involving formal applications and interviews were flouted and skill requirements waived for certain appointments. Political influence was also used to favour particular candidates in transfer and promotion decisions. Some of these were relatively junior positions for fresh graduates. Other appointments were more strategic and at more senior levels; these were particularly influential within the customs and excise department since politically appointed staff would be in a position to waive or reduce duty requirements or undervalue shipping consignments for patrons with influence and leverage. Officials who did not comply with political expectations were vulnerable to transfer or failed to secure promotion. Such influence was not limited to routine appointments.

In many ways, influence in appointments is to be expected in government agencies when patronage prevails in the political system. But politically motivated promotions and transfers erode incentives for regularly appointed staff and create rivalry in the organisation. The scope for corruption intensifies as jobs are treated as opportunities for rent-seeking.[4] The form of autonomy granted to the URA appears to have aggravated the problem. In the words of Therkildsen (2004: 2), 'Paradoxically, the more autonomy a revenue service has, the more it seems to attract political attention, which in turn may threaten revenue autonomy'.

Strong political support is often claimed to be a critical factor in the initiation and successful implementation of governance reforms. President Museveni was personally very supportive of the proposal to create an autonomous revenue body and used his authority to counter ministerial and political resistance. But the President became increasingly hostile to the URA from the mid-1990s, reflected in critical comments and speeches that were reported in the media. He publicly railed against corruption in the URA and blamed officials for failing to defend the introduction of value added tax (VAT) in the face of strikes and protests. There was increasing recourse to the special revenue protection services under the Office of the President to enforce tax collection, employing heavy-handed methods in the form of raids on traders and confiscation of goods. These developments served to undermine the URA's credibility and sap the motivation of senior staff. The erosion of high-level political support weakened URA's ability to withstand political interference from other quarters and undermined the momentum of reform (Therkildsen, 2004: 15).

Another ingredient of successful institutional reform is the design of management and internal governance structures. The URA's semi-autonomous status was intended to provide its management with authority and independence in decision-making as a basis for determining an appropriate mix of structures and incentives for optimising tax collection. But senior management did not wield sufficient independence from the MOFPED officials who dominated the Board and sought to exert influence over routine decisions concerning staffing, remuneration, and administration. A highly interventionist Board undermined the authority of the CG and detracted attention from larger policy issues.

A major source of organisational inefficiency lay in the process of recruitment adopted at the outset. The wholesale transfer of ministry staff to the newly created URA followed by selective weeding out of non-performers ensured that the majority of staff were civil servants and that a bureaucratic mindset continued to pervade the organisation. Many unproductive staff remained in the organisation by virtue of capacity constraints. In particular, the scope for hiring new technical and managerial specialists was constrained by a shortage of suitably qualified graduates with finance and accountancy training. Accordingly, the new agency was created with a dearth of leadership and management skills, which contrasted markedly with the new technocratic elite being groomed in MOFPED. Recruitment of expatriates and foreign technical experts proved to be a temporary palliative, since few remained in post for long. By the late 1990s, trained graduates with appropriate qualifications were no longer attracted by URA pay and conditions and preferred to join the private sector with its expanding opportunities. Moreover, there has been considerable turnover of staff in senior positions on account of dismissals, resignations, politically motivated transfers, and a recruitment freeze pending the findings of a corruption enquiry in 2004. Frequent changes in organisational structures weakened institutional memory and management coherence.

These three problems – the erosion of autonomy, the loss of political momentum, and the failure to build a technocratic cadre – are the mirror image of the factors often believed to be essential for successful reform implementation. These ingredients were present at the inception of the URA and helped to explain its early success. But these very factors result from failures in political and institutional design and expose the limits of this approach in a political context shaped by informal institutional imperatives of patronage and personal rule. In the case of the URA, these problems contributed to increasing organisational atrophy and loss of reform momentum.

A chronic manifestation of this growing institutional malaise was the growth and deepening of corruption, one of the very problems that a semi-autonomous tax authority was intended to redress.[5] Although the problem was already evident by the mid-1990s, a decade later it had become chronic, pervasive, and well organised (Therkildsen, 2004: 10–11). There are several explanatory factors for the resurfacing of corruption in the URA. One study found that political interference in tax administration was ranked above all other causes of corruption by URA staff. Inadequate pay was also a significant factor, especially for junior support and collection staff who identified this as the dominant motivation (Mwanje, 2003: 99). Political intrusion in recruitment and transfers provided opportunities for staff to solicit kickbacks for tax evasion and discretionary treatment in tax assessment in the knowledge that they would have political protection in the event of an enquiry. Such behaviour provoked similar responses from regularly appointed staff who often came under pressure to indulge in malfeasance in return for a share of the benefits.

Pay and conditions also contributed to declining performance. The falling real value of URA salaries and substantial differentials between junior and senior officials were a source of resentment, leading staff to indulge in corrupt practices to maintain the lifestyle to which they had become accustomed or simply to supplement low salaries. Weaknesses in surveillance systems and sanctions were also a contributory factor, reflected in the relatively small number of officials who were sanctioned or dismissed as a consequence of investigations. Growing concern in the media and from foreign donors over the magnitude and extent of corruption in the URA prompted the government to appoint an independent enquiry headed by Justice Sebutinde in 2002.[6]

The main lesson of the URA experience is that autonomy per se does not guarantee independence or increase efficiency, confirming growing recognition of the limitations of the enclave approach to reform (Devas *et al.*, 2001). Autonomy in the absence of effective mechanisms for ensuring accountability and in a political context characterised by the dominance of patrimonial compulsions provides an inauspicious context for reform. Generous salaries can generate perverse incentives without contributing to enhanced motivation and performance on a sustained basis. Autonomy in the absence of accountability provides opportunities for political influence over appointments and transfers in response to the lure of enhanced status and superior conditions. Political influence over staffing decisions has proved to be a source of growing corruption and inefficiency, in turn undermining the early achievements of the URA experiment and threatening the fragile revenue base of the state over the longer run.

Anti-corruption Measures: The Politics of Accountability

The elimination of corruption was one of the objectives of the NRM's Ten-Point Programme developed in the mid-1980s during the struggle against the Obote II regime. The problem had become endemic in the public service on account of very poor salaries and conditions and the lack of effective accountability and oversight mechanisms. The prevalence of corruption was a key consideration in the government's Civil Service Reform Programme and the creation of the URA and other semi-autonomous agencies. The aim of these reforms was to create a living wage and an ethos of efficient and transparent government, and to devolve implementation to executive agencies that could establish systems and build incentives as a means of discouraging corrupt practices.

As an integral part of the effort to combat corruption, the government strengthened existing institutional mechanisms and created a series of new institutions responsible for ensuring probity and integrity in the public service. The former included the Office of the Auditor General, the Department of Public Prosecutions (DPP), and the Criminal Investigation Department (CID). Years of neglect and under-funding had weakened their effectiveness and their legitimacy had become compromised by corruption and inefficiency. The NRM government sought to reinvigorate these institutions through infusion of financial resources and capacity-building, largely funded by aid donors. Many legal measures were introduced in the 1990s to strengthen the mandate and powers of these institutions.

The Office of the Auditor General (AG) is responsible for auditing public accounts and submitting reports to parliament for scrutiny and deliberation through the Public Accounts Committee (PAC). It is a semi-autonomous body established under the constitution. Its reports are shared with the DPP and the Inspectorate of Government (IoG) for follow-up action and investigations. The AG is appointed by the President, who has the power to remove the post-holder on the grounds of misconduct or incompetence. The AG has some degree of independence in formulating a programme of work, but only to a limited extent in staff recruitment and appointments, which are largely determined by the Public Service Commission in line with practice in other government departments. The AG's budget is submitted to MOFPED, which then proposes an allocation that is endorsed by the cabinet.

The work of the Office of the Auditor General is hampered by a number of limitations. Despite its constitutional status, the independence of the AG is compromised both by the power of the President in appointments and by the lack of budgetary autonomy. Its work is further impeded by a lack of suitably qualified staff, especially experienced accountants, and its inability to make decisions on staff recruitment and retention. Management practices are derived from civil service norms and are incompatible with the demands of a modern and efficient audit body. The work of the AG is also held back by inadequate financial resources.

Another area of concern is the ability of the legislature to review and recommend action on the AG's reports. In the late 1980s and early 1990s there were significant delays in reporting to parliament through the PAC with backlogs of several years, which limited scope for identifying and acting on corrupt practices. The AG lacked qualified staff and used out-of-date methods for collecting and analysing public expenditure data. Over time, the AG was able to recruit more capable staff with accountancy qualifications and to modernise systems through computerisation and the development of modern auditing methods. The AG's reports are now produced on time but the PAC has yet to catch up on the backlog of reports. The backlog reduces the effectiveness of parliamentary oversight, because it becomes more difficult for the PAC to recommend action and call public officials to account when the reports refer to expenditures committed in past financial years.[7] While the PAC has called for action against departmental accounting officers (usually permanent secretaries) by the IoG and DPP, the follow-up has been slow and intermittent, with few prosecutions and limited recovery of funds. The PAC lacks office support and clerical staff, further reducing its effectiveness and ability to catch up on the backlog. A further problem is that of supplementary budgets, where special appropriations are made for additional expenditures on items such as defence and public administration without effective parliamentary scrutiny (Mugasha *et al.*, 2002; Van Arkadie, 2003). It is widely recognised that the PAC is ill-equipped to deal with the scale of the problem and that it lacks political support at the highest level.

The Inspectorate of Government (IoG) was one of the key institutions created by the NRM government to address problems of corruption. It was established in 1986 as an independent institution charged with promoting adherence to the rule of law in public administration and responsibility for eliminating corruption and abuse of authority and public office, reporting to the President. The 1995 Constitution strengthened its powers of investigation, arrest, and prosecution, and increased its autonomy, requiring it to report directly to parliament. The IoG is also responsible for implementing the Leadership Code of Conduct, which was initially promulgated in 1992 and affirmed in the constitution, requiring government officials and MPs to declare their income, assets, and liabilities on a yearly basis. This provision provides the IoG with the powers to enforce the code and prosecute officials found guilty of corruption and abuse of public office.

The IoG was restructured in 2001 to strengthen its work and improve its effectiveness. Information technology has been employed to improve its speed and efficiency in handling cases. A new Inspectorate of Government Act in 2002 strengthened the power and independence of the IoG and it is now funded directly through a parliamentary vote providing it with greater budgetary autonomy.

However, the reorganisation of the IoG and the strengthening of its powers through new legislation have not markedly improved its performance. Its record in identifying and prosecuting corruption cases remains poor and its legitimacy and effectiveness remain open to question. Judicial action on cases furnished by the IoG is marked by delays, and many case reports are returned as they lack essential pieces of information and evidence. It suffers from resource constraints in terms of inadequate budgets and lack of skilled staff and vehicles and office support. It has proved difficult to recruit and retain staff with appropriate skills and expertise, especially lawyers. This feeds into a vicious circle of inadequate resources, poor staffing calibre, reduced efficiency and effectiveness, low rates of prosecution, and diminished credibility.

High-level political support for the IoG has also waned. The President no longer provides strong public support for the institution. Close ties with the

President's family have not prevented erosion in its political status. Government hostility to the IoG was evident from its submission to the Constitutional Review Commission (CRC) in 2003, in which it proposed amendments designed to curb its power and autonomy. There have also been calls from senior political figures and presidential advisers for the removal of the IoG's power to enforce the implementation of the Leadership Code following its decision to take action against influential politicians who had refused to submit their declaration. The most plausible reason for diminishing political support is that the imperative of maintaining a core support base for the Movement detracts from a political commitment to tackling high-level corruption through empowering the IoG and other institutions of restraint. The work of the IoG is therefore undermined by a combination of capacity and resource constraints and a lack of sustained political support.

Aid donors grew increasingly restive in the late 1990s over the government's poor performance in countering corruption and pressed for a more concerted response. Concern was also prompted by several high-profile corruption cases involving close relatives of the President (Tangri & Mwenda, 2001). The problems encountered by institutions responsible for ensuring administrative probity and transparency and the government's poor record on addressing corruption came in for particular criticism from aid donors but these were largely attributed by the government to a lack of effective coordination rather than deficiencies in administrative capacity and political will. It was argued that the government was well served by a panoply of institutions with an anti-corruption remit, but that these had overlapping responsibilities and jurisdictions and did not have effective means of working together.

The Directorate of Ethics and Integrity (DEI) was created in 1998 following a review led by the Vice-President (on the recommendation of the President) to look into the functioning of existing anti-corruption bodies. The DEI is charged with responsibility for setting policy and standards, capacity-building, monitoring, and coordination of official anti-corruption bodies. The creation of a central coordinating institution that would report to the President was intended to raise the profile of anti-corruption efforts in the government.

Despite lofty ambitions, the DEI has suffered from similar problems to the more specialised anti-corruption bodies. Difficulties of recruiting professionals with appropriate skills emanate from poor public service pay and conditions and the disincentives arising from short-term contracts with no pension entitlement. It has also proved difficult to retain graduate lawyers who are attracted by superior pay and conditions in the private sector. The DEI also has severe resource constraints, reflecting its marginal political status and inability to secure budget commitments commensurate with its role. Budget shortfalls have been partially augmented by donor technical assistance and financial support for office infrastructure.

While officials point to some success in coordination and in preventing appointments of corrupt officials, the work of the DEI is also hampered by the poor performance of the agencies responsible for investigation and prosecution of corruption. The CID of the Ugandan police is responsible for investigation of criminal cases, while the DPP is responsible for preparing prosecution cases on behalf of the government. These agencies face similar problems to those experienced by the IoG and the DEI, and the effectiveness of their work is compromised by institutional and capacity constraints. The CID is not computerised, suffers from poor record-keeping, has limited transport facilities, and lacks personnel with the appropriate forensic and legal skills. The DPP also suffers from resource constraints in the form of poor remuneration and benefits, and chronic under-staffing. These problems further undermine the credibility of the government's anti-corruption efforts and are compounded in high-profile corruption cases where there is witness intimidation and a lack of effective enforcement.

All these initiatives have had a limited impact on overall levels of corruption. Uganda is rated among the most corrupt countries in the world by Transparency International, ranked 117 out of 133 countries surveyed for the Corruption Perceptions Index in 2003. Public perceptions testify to the scale and intensity of the problem and the perceived limitations of official anti-corruption initiatives. The 1998 National Integrity Survey, commissioned by the IoG, found very high levels of corruption in agencies responsible for delivering public services, especially in the police and judiciary. The majority of respondents thought that low salaries and delays in payment were the principal causes of corruption, as well as outright greed (Ruzindana *et al.*, 1998).[8] Similar results were generated in a follow-up survey in early 2003. Media allegations of the corrupt business activities of senior ministers and close family members of the President further erode public confidence that the government is serious about honouring its ostensible commitment to combating corruption.

The central problem in Uganda's anti-corruption efforts lies not in the absence of institutions for tackling the problem, but rather in their systematic marginalisation and consequent inability to investigate and prosecute officials and politicians at the highest level of government. In narrow institutional terms Uganda's anti-corruption effort might be interpreted as a success, reflected in an impressive array of organisations with power and responsibility for investigation, prosecution, and punishment. However, evidence on their performance in curbing the level of corruption measured through the number of successful prosecutions and dismissals points to a consistent record of underachievement.

Corruption has a high political profile and the President has publicly associated himself with anti-corruption efforts. The more cynical commentators allege that the government's high-profile anti-corruption efforts are designed to assuage donor criticism of its failure to address the root causes of the problem rather than emanating from conviction and political will (Flanary & Watt, 1999). The problem of political will is compounded by the shortage of material and human resources facing all the anti-corruption agencies. All face staff shortages and budgetary constraints and are poorly equipped (Watt *et al.*, 1999). The lack or fragility of constitutional safeguards weakens their autonomy and independence, rendering them vulnerable to political influence. Corruption is a manifestation of the political compulsions of patrimonialism, taking the form of a reward for political loyalty and a division of spoils designed to maintain the support base of the Movement. In view of the evident reluctance of the government to tackle the problem with conviction, the scope for curbing corruption and fostering accountability through under-resourced and politically marginalised institutions will remain extremely limited.

Conclusions

The three cases of governance reforms in Uganda surveyed in this article – civil service reform, the creation of a semi-autonomous revenue authority, and anti-corruption agencies – share a number of common features. First, they have all passed through a similar trajectory in their implementation: initial success in achieving a number of key objectives followed by a loss of momentum, or reversals. Second, the institutional features that appear to account for initial success also help to explain their susceptibility to a process of unravelling; namely, strong political support to technocratic or bureaucratic elites with some degree of insulation from political and societal interests through the creation of specialised, semi-autonomous agencies responsible for reform implementation. Third, the principal explanation for stalled reform (or even reversal of gains) lies in the imperative of preserving the institutional foundations of neo-patrimonial politics.

Initial success was evident in a number of outcomes. Success in civil service reform resulted from downsizing and rationalising the bureaucracy, reflected in a reduction in the number of civil servants and ministries. In the case of the URA, the key achievement was increased tax revenues. The main result of anti-corruption efforts has been the creation of a series of institutions charged with responsibility for various aspects of this work, but with modest success in prosecuting civil servants found guilty of corrupt practices. And yet in each case the momentum of reform has not been sustained. The objective of a minimum living wage for civil servants is far from being realised and the bureaucracy is once again expanding, thereby increasing the budgetary share of public administration. The rate of growth in tax revenues has flattened out and corruption in the URA has sharply increased. The anti-corruption agencies lack resources and capacity, in turn undermining their effectiveness. The legitimacy of these institutions has come under question in the face of a low rate of prosecutions and the failure to check large-scale corruption by senior political figures connected to the Movement.

While there are characteristics common to all three sets of governance reforms in terms of political vulnerability and weaknesses in institutional design, there are also some perceptible differences. These relate to the varying impact of political and public servant incentives and of citizen engagement. The political incentive, for instance, is greatest with regard to civil service reform with its promise to build state capacity and curb the potentially antagonistic influence of bureaucrats appointed under previous regimes. Successful anti-corruption measures, on the other hand, could undermine support for the regime from highly placed officials and politicians, so do not tend to engender political motivation. By contrast, while civil service and anti-corruption reforms both pose a high level of disincentive to individual civil servants, who stand to lose either their jobs or opportunities for rent-seeking, revenue reform offers high incentives through significant increases in salaries and kudos. Anti-corruption measures do, however, represent a high incentive for the engagement of citizens who will no longer be forced to pay bribes for services. But citizens stand to gain little from either civil service reform, which is largely structural, or from taxation reform, since relatively few Ugandans pay taxes.

Common to all three reform initiatives, however, was that strong initial political support for them from the President proved to be short-lived. Once the initial, more visible, objectives had been achieved, presidential attention turned to other priorities, such as service delivery outcomes and the war in the north. Ostensible commitment to governance reform is offset by public presidential dissatisfaction with the slow pace of reform, the weakness of institutions established to spearhead the reform effort, and the perceived intransigence of civil servants. There are several possible explanations for this behaviour. One is the perception that governance reforms do not generate political dividends. Rather, successful implementation of structural reforms in the civil service and anti-corruption agencies has the potential to alienate civil servants, by reducing their access to rents and the fruits of office, even though the opportunity to curb bureaucratic power was politically attractive in the short term. While certain types of governance reforms generate some amount of public goodwill, they do not provide an assured means of galvanising political support. Second, it has been argued that presidential support for reforms was a response to the expectations of aid donors who increasingly demanded evidence of commitment to governance reforms, especially with regard to anti-corruption measures. Third, presidential support can be seen as an outcome of a shrewd political calculus in which political self-preservation was a dominant consideration.

However, the most compelling explanation for the slowing of reform momentum and weakening of the institutions responsible for implementing reforms lies in the politics of patrimonialism. Political commitment was undoubtedly a motivating factor in the decision to pursue a governance reform agenda at a time when the Movement was broad-based in character and committed to a state-led project of rehabilitation, growth, and poverty reduction. The evidence surveyed here leads to the conclusion that the institutional architecture of governance reforms was shaped by political considerations, and took the form of autonomy and both insulation from civil society and bureaucratic self-interest, and that these were vulnerable to capture by dominant political constituencies within the Movement. These constituencies emerge from the neo-patrimonial character of Ugandan political culture in which personalised rule and patronage relations founded on kinship, family, and community are the key ingredients. The design and trajectory of governance reforms directly reflects the shifting basis of neo-patrimonialism, as the compulsions of preserving political power increasingly take precedence over benign presidential interventionism.

The impact of neo-patrimonial politics in the governance domain is manifest in the use of the state machinery to reward supporters (through appointments and positions in semi-autonomous agencies and commissions), the expansion of the political bureaucracy, and the systematic under-resourcing of anti-corruption agencies and official commissions of enquiry. Political incentives for reform do not emanate from the potential attractiveness of improved governance per se, but from fresh opportunities for exercising power, influence, and remuneration emanating from new institutional configurations governed by patronage considerations. The no-party Movement system offered few checks and balances and facilitated the re-emergence of a new form of patrimonial politics with perverse implications for the sustainability of governance reforms, though this may change with the reintroduction of multi-party politics.

The lessons arising from the Ugandan experience may well have broader implications for the design and implementation of governance reforms in comparable political environments elsewhere, despite the uniqueness of the Movement system. Political commitment and donor support were integral to the early success of governance reforms. High-level political commitment is clearly an essential prerequisite for initiating reform, but this simultaneously presents a potent source of vulnerability in a political culture with a powerful legacy of authoritarianism and personal rule. When political priorities change and the politics of regime maintenance prevail over the impetus for reforms their sustainability becomes increasingly problematic. The Ugandan experience highlights the difficulty of sustaining successful reform initiatives over a long period of time in a context of patrimonialism and personal rule in which benign intentions can be compromised by other political prerogatives.

The Ugandan experience also raises a key challenge for adherents of reform: what kinds of political institutions, incentive systems, and institutional design features sustain successful governance reforms? The personal commitment of a political leader like President Museveni cannot be assured over an extended time period and governance reforms require a broader political constituency to ensure their sustainability. A more active and engaged civil society would help to engender greater accountability on the part of top bureaucrats and political leaders. In theory, a more competitive party system should provide opportunities for greater deliberation and oversight of reform implementation. But before the advent of multi-party elections, the narrowing of the Movement's support base, ongoing controls on the activities of civil society organisations, and the limitations on competitive party politics all ran counter to this possibility. The new multi-party dispensation might deepen rather than erode patrimonial politics as newly mobilised constituencies seek to access the benefits that were formerly the exclusive preserve of politicians and officials associated with the Movement. Restoring the legitimacy and capacity of state institutions will be a major challenge under conditions of enhanced political competition, in which autonomy and insulation are balanced by effective accountability and oversight to prevent further loss of reform momentum.

Notes

1. A detailed exploration of the politics of the Movement and neo-patrimonialism is beyond the scope of this article. For details see Mamdani (1996); (Chabal & Daloz, 1999).
2. The data for this study derive from 40 interviews with government officials, donor representatives and academics in Uganda in March 2004, and secondary materials in the form of government and aid donor reports.
3. According to one source, 72 appointments were made for political reasons to a variety of positions in the URA from the mid-1990s, in which influence rather than merit dictated the terms of the appointment.
4. Interviewees claimed a close correspondence between politically appointed staff and the propensity for corruption.
5. A detailed analysis can be found in Fjeldstad *et al.* (2003), and the survey conducted by Mwanje (2003).
6. The commission's report was submitted in early 2004 but had not yet been made public by the end of 2006.
7. For instance, parliament only initiated debate on the PAC's report relating to the financial year ending June 2000 nearly four years later, in April 2004.
8. *Uganda National Integrity Survey 1998: Final Report*, submitted by CIET International to the Inspectorate of Government, Kampala, August.

References

Campos, J. E. & Pradhan, S. (2005) A framework for studying governance reforms at the country level, in *Economic Growth in the 1990s: Learning from a Decade of Reform* (Washington, DC: World Bank).

Chabal, P. & Daloz, J.-P. (1999) *Africa Works: Disorder as a Political Instrument* (Oxford: James Currey).

Devas, N., Delay, S. & Hubbard, M. (2001) Revenue authorities: are they the right vehicle for improved tax administration?, *Public Administration and Development*, 21(3), pp. 211–222.

Fjeldstad, O., Kolstad, I. & Lange, S. (2003) *Autonomy, Incentives and Patronage: A Study of Corruption in the Tanzania and Uganda Revenue Authorities*, CMI Reports 2003: 9 (Bergen: Christian Michelsen Institute).

Flanary, R. & Watt, D. (1999) The state of corruption: a case study of Uganda, *Third World Quarterly*, 20(3), pp. 515–536.

Francis, P. & James, R. (2003) Balancing rural poverty reduction and citizen participation: the contradictions of Uganda's decentralization programme, *World Development*, 31(2), pp. 325–337.

Goetz, A. M. (2007) Manoeuvring past clientelism: institutions and incentives to generate constituencies in support of governance reforms, *Commonwealth and Comparative Politics*, 45(4), pp. 403–424.

Harvey, C. & Robinson, M. (1995) *Economic Reform and Political Liberalisation in Uganda*, IDS Research Report 29 (Brighton: Institute of Development Studies).

Hickey, S. (2003) *The Politics of Staying Poor in Uganda*, CPRC Working Paper 37 (Manchester: Institute of Development Policy and Management, Chronic Poverty Research Centre).

Kiragu, K. & Mukandala, R. (2005) *Politics and Tactics in Public Sector Reforms: The Dynamics of Public Service Pay in Africa* (Dar es Salaam: Dar es Salaam University Press).

Kjaer, A. M. (2004) 'Old brooms can sweep too!' An overview of rulers and public sector reforms in Uganda, Tanzania and Kenya, *Journal of Modern African Studies*, 42(3), pp. 1–25.

Langseth, P. (1995) Civil service reform in Uganda: lessons learned, *Public Administration and Development*, 15(1), pp. 365–390.

Mamdani, M. (1996) *Citizen and Subject: Contemporary Africa and the Legacy of Late Colonialism* (London: James Currey).

Mugasha, F., Kassami, C., Van Arkadie, B. & Berger, A.-M. (2002) *Final Report of the Committee to Advise the President on More Effective Public Administration Budgeting* (Kampala: Office of the Prime Minister and Ministry of Finance, Planning and Economic Development).

Mwanje, D. M. (2003) Causes of corruption in Uganda revenue authority, *URA Fiscal Bulletin*, 2(1), pp. 83–123.

Ruzindana, A., Langseth, P. & Gakwadi, A. (1998) *Fighting Corruption in Uganda: The Process of Building a National Integrity System* (Kampala: Fountain).

Tangri, R. & Mwenda, A. (2001) Corruption and cronyism in Uganda's privatisation in the 1990s, *African Affairs*, 100(398), pp. 117–133.

Therkildsen, O. (2004) *Autonomous Tax Administration in Sub-Saharan Africa: The Case of Uganda Revenue Authority*, mimeo.

Van Arkadie, B. (2003) *A Report on Public Administration and the PEAP Revision* (Kampala: Office of the Prime Minister and the Ministry of Finance, Planning and Economic Development).

Watt, D., Flanary, R. & Theobald, R. (1999) Democratisation or democratisation of corruption? The case of Uganda, *Commonwealth and Comparative Politics*, 37(3), pp. 37–64.

Governance Reform and Institutional Change in Brazil: Federalism and Tax

AARON SCHNEIDER

Institute of Development Studies, Sussex, UK

The concept of governance is increasingly entering the practice and lexicon of development. This focus is not completely new. Decolonisation during the post-World War II period removed foreign-controlled coercive authority from the South, and the challenge of constructing authoritative, effective, and legitimate institutions rose high on the development agenda. For Huntington and others writing at the time, 'the most important distinction among countries concerns not their form of government but their degree of government' (Huntington, 1968: 1).

Current attention to governance is different, but it is plagued by some of the same problems. Most important is that we do not recognise change until it has already happened. As a result, we are forced to look backwards, after the fact, and attempt to compare successful cases. This creates obvious problems of selection bias, and in response we might try to identify cases of non-reform for comparison. Yet, this is extremely difficult; after all, one cannot know if a reform was meant to happen but did not. To get beyond this problem, the current paper explores two episodes of attempted governance reform in the same country over the same years: federalism reform and tax reform. In improving governance, the first reform succeeded and the second failed.

What does it mean to succeed or fail at improving governance? This is not an easy question to answer, as the concept of governance itself is essentially contested. Still, a workable definition for the purposes at hand builds on the notion of governance as state-building. Governance is 'the manner in which the State exercises and acquires authority' (Campos & Pradhan, 2003: 1). This can be disaggregated into two dimensions: capacity and accountability. 'Capacity' refers to the bureaucratic, technical, fiscal, and coercive authority of government leaders to impose their will on private and public actors. 'Accountability' refers to the mechanisms of linkage that allow 'principals' within society to monitor and control the actions of government 'agents'. Changes in one or both of these dimensions constitute governance reform, and changes in both constitute an improvement in governance.

Two Patterns of Change in Brazilian Institutions

Governance reform in Brazil produced improvements in capacity and accountability during the 1990s. These improvements were necessary because the institutions inherited from the military regime that left power in 1985 were imperfectly suited to a democratic opening and economic liberalisation. Yet, there was no guarantee that governance would improve, and it did not improve evenly in all areas. In one case studied here, the case of tax reform, adjustments were made within existing institutional arrangements and governance improved only marginally. In the other case, the Fiscal Responsibility Law of 2000, the adjustments brought about pressure that ultimately led to the elimination of existing institutions, the forging of a new social pact, and the construction of a new federal relationship.

The Fiscal Responsibility Law reflected the tipping point of a cumulative process that eventually breached a threshold in Brazilian federalism. Reform was the culmination of a series of minor shifts that fundamentally renegotiated the interests and relative powers of parties to the federal covenant. These marginal and incremental changes did the hard work of weakening certain actors, strengthening others, altering preferences, eroding previous institutions, and setting the architecture of a new federalism. A particular historical moment, marked by external economic crisis, tipped the balance, and it was possible to establish new institutions codified to meet the requirements of the Fiscal Responsibility Law.

Tax reform was also a slow and gradual process of change in which Machiavellian manoeuvres shifted actors, interests, and relative powers. Yet, in tax reform, a new social pact was not possible, legacies of the military regime and the transition to democracy remained rigid and relatively difficult to change, and the reforms that did occur expanded revenues and modernised some practices, but they were unable to tackle basic problems of inefficiency and inequality.

Degrees and Kinds of Change

To explain why governance reforms occur, this paper builds on rational choice and historical institutionalist approaches. Both argue that governance institutions rest on durable pacts in which actors agree to formal and informal rules that limit their behaviour, especially in terms of limiting potential conflicts. From a rational choice approach, pacts are chosen because they are efficient (North, 1991). From a historical institutional approach, pacts are the result of decisions taken at moments of critical juncture, bounded by the weakening of prior institutions and the introduction of new institutions that last for long periods (Collier & Collier, 1991). Both approaches consider changing patterns of governance as the dynamic of various actors pacting, un-pacting, and re-pacting.

Here, we are primarily concerned with two kinds of governance improvement: within-institution change and wholesale institution change. Within-institution changes are limited in scope to the boundaries of existing institutions. Significant policy consequences can result, but there is no fundamental altering of the rules of the game and no large-scale change in governance. No new actors enter political debate; there is no significant change in actor power and interests; and all strategies simply adjust at the margins. Most importantly, this leaves intact the institutions themselves (Thelen, 2003).

Within-institution changes differ from wholesale institution changes. Wholesale changes are bigger, in that they produce much greater improvements in the capacity and accountability of the state, i.e. its governance. Yet, wholesale change is also different in kind; one set of institutions replaces another. This both increases governance and also alters the way in which governance operates.

The triggers of both kinds of change can be both external and internal. For example, exogenously driven economic crisis, world events, or external pressure can cause ruptures, forcing institutions to change. Also, endogenous events such as internal decay and Machiavellian manoeuvres by different actors can shift preferences and relative powers.

One source of change has received particular attention in the larger literature, and that is local ownership. Such ownership is evident in both cases of reform in Brazil, yet only one of the reforms met with success. It was only when alliances and strategies produced a new social pact that wholesale change in institutions could occur. Ownership may have been necessary for such a new social pact to emerge, but it was certainly not sufficient.

The notion of necessary and sufficient causes deserves additional consideration. The two cases here are difficult to analyse for several reasons. First, changes were gradual and incremental. Such a rhythm is difficult to recognise, as the changes only become visible when some threshold is passed (Pierson, 2000). Further, the incremental steps, which make up the bulk of the discussion below, are in no way independent. No single action or cause was sufficient to produce reform. Rather, each incremental step was necessary but not sufficient.[1] Finally, the nature of success deserves some attention. In both cases, successful reform is described as a wholesale change in governance in which both accountability and capacity have increased. The Fiscal Responsibility Law capped a process by which government gained new capacity to coordinate sub-national actors and government became more accountable to citizens. In tax, enhanced capacity mobilised greater resources from society, but that enhanced capacity came without increases in accountability, simply tightening the screws on already taxed sectors and coming at the cost of decreased efficiency and equity.

Wholesale Institutional Change – A New Pact around Fiscal Responsibility

In the last few years, Brazil has achieved a high degree of fiscal transparency, together with major improvements in the management of public finances. The cornerstone of these achievements has been the enactment in May 2000 of the Fiscal Responsibility Law, which sets out for all levels of government fiscal rules designed to ensure medium-term fiscal sustainability, and strict transparency requirements to underpin the effectiveness and credibility of such rules (International Monetary Fund, 2001: 1).

The Fiscal Responsibility Law of 2000 marked a change in the nature of Brazilian federalism. It can be understood as the culmination of a repeated series of interactions between central government, the executive branch, Congress, and sub-national units, especially states. Few who looked at Brazil in 1988 might have suspected that the federal order would be completely changed in little over a decade. The actors and institutions that favoured retaining a chaotic federal system of powerful states seemed unlikely to change, and the few actors who wished to establish a degree of fiscal coordination were weak. Over the course of the 1990s, however, actors altered their positions, relative powers changed, and strategies adjusted. Over time, this undermined the pact that sustained the previous federalism arrangement, and new arrangements were codified in the Fiscal Responsibility Law.

For the designers and supporters of the law, it marked a sea change in the nature of Brazilian federalism. Instead of federalism as a bargain to hold together an otherwise fragmenting union, federalism came to be a tool to manage public finance efficiently and effectively (Stepan, 2000). This signals more than establishing legal prohibitions; rather, there has been a change in the nature of federalism itself. Such a change was only possible through a social pact that could wipe away old institutions and establish new ones.[2]

The current analysis views the Fiscal Responsibility Law as the tipping point in a series of cumulative, gradual changes that crystallised new federal institutions. Where we begin this story of gradual change is somewhat arbitrary, but a clear cut-point can be identified in the 1988 Constitution. That Constitution gave sub-national governments significant power and resources. In particular, governors' control over state enterprises and banks had national macroeconomic implications. The political power of governors was articulated at the national level by state delegations in Congress and the Senate, and the Senate as an institution held important powers in relation to the executive in the area of sub-national debt. Potential restraints on these sub-national actors were absent, as electoral laws and political practices produced multi-member districts, undisciplined parties, and a weak civil society. It is this period that most observers are referring to when they characterise Brazil as a 'demos-constraining', extreme federalism.

The fiscal scenario of the federal system was extremely precarious. Many of the states had made their own situations even more difficult by locking themselves into major spending initiatives, partly to cover reductions in federal investments, and partly as a result of electoral cycles during the transition to democracy producing seven elections in 10 years (1985, 1986, 1988, 1989, 1990, 1992, and 1994). The fiscal impact of the hiring binges associated with these elections was compounded in the 1988 Constitution, which placed all public employees on regulated labour contracts that included complicated termination and generous pensions. Pensions were also extended to rural workers, and many states found themselves carrying some of this burden as well. As a result, several states found themselves with over 90 per cent of their budget dedicated to public sector personnel (Varsano, 2003).

To finance their expansion, the states turned to temporary stopgaps. They indexed taxes to inflation while delaying and failing to index many expenditures. They also floated financial assets through state banks that essentially allowed governors to give loans to themselves (Giambiagi & Além, 2001). At least for a time, they could cover themselves with increasing transfers from the federal government, but their debts soon ballooned and they defaulted.

This dismal scenario changed gradually and incrementally. The first major shift occurred in 1994, with the Real Plan, which stabilised the currency and defeated inflation, which had reached over 1000 per cent per year. Yet, the Real Plan, which secured fiscal stability for the central government, greatly undermined the practices that sub-national units had used to sustain themselves. For example, by raising interest rates by 60 per cent in three years, the Central Bank sustained the value of the currency, but also greatly increased the burden of state government debts (Alston *et al.*, 2004). Also, the end of inflation meant that states could not inflate away their debts. Finally, the Real Plan further damaged state finances as the central government retained more of the revenues that were meant to be shared with the states (Giambiagi & Além, 2001).

Governments were forced to depend even more significantly on transfers from the central government and new credit operations, often from fragile state banks. Sub-national debt increased by 85 per cent from 1990 to 1996 and almost doubled as a portion of total national debt (Mora & Varsano, 2001). As the states fell deeper and deeper into debt, they turned to the central government for help.

Two early crises were characterised by state debts to the central government (1989) and to federal institutions such as the housing and savings bank (1993). The workouts after these crises included renegotiation of debt burdens, rescheduling of payments, lowering of interest rates, and some pressure to privatise and cut expenses. For some observers, these workouts seemed to be incentives to bad behaviour and typical of moral hazard problems (Dillinger, 1995; Dillinger & Webb, 1999; Perry & Webb, 1999; Rodden *et al.*, 2003; Ter-Minassian, 1997). What these observers failed to recognise was the shifting terrain of relative powers.

A third crisis after 1994 made clear that the relative powers of states and central government had shifted. After the Real Plan, states mostly owed debts to their own state banks and to private banks on short-term state bonds and loans in anticipation of revenues. During the 1970s and 1980s, state banks had financed poles of investment, but the transition to democracy had encouraged governors to use their power over state bank directors to secure funds for current expenses. Many of the bonds issued through these banks were issued at high interest rates on short-term, even overnight, markets, and states eventually defaulted, causing stress on national macroeconomic management. The largest states and municipalities had the most privileged access to financial markets, but their unpayable state bonds reached over R$30 billion (approximately US$25 billion in 1997) (Goldfajn & Guardia, 2003).

In 1997, a new framework for debt workouts was established. The framework was followed by agreements with 24 states for US$82 billion, with 30-year repayment schedules and low, fixed interest rates. The ceiling on debt service was also set somewhat generously, not to pass 15 per cent of current revenues (Rezende & Afonso, 2002: 16). The law also established ceilings for personnel, and targets for growth in revenues and privatisation (Guimarães, 2004). Failure to meet conditions could be punished with retention of state constitutional transfers.

The difference between this debt workout and previous ones was that state governments were significantly weaker. In the early bailouts, the federal government negotiated with states en masse, largely setting the same conditions for all states and negotiating partly through the Senate. After 1994, the President and Ministry of Finance sought to divide the states by negotiating with each governor individually. In particular, the large states were targeted early, strengthening central government's hand in later negotiations with smaller states (Webb, 2004).

These bargaining strategies were reflected in the terms of the workouts. They were linked to fiscal adjustment programmes in which states were required to secure a down-payment on debt equal to 20 per cent of the total. In general, funds for this down-payment were to come from privatisation, and the federal government pressured states to privatise their state banks. Within a few years, almost all state banks were either made purely developmental banks or eliminated entirely. To this end, the President had used decree power in 1996 to establish a fund Programa de Estímulo à Redução do Setor Público no Sistema Financeiro (PROES) which eventually spent R$62 billion to eliminate the bad debts of state banks and prepare them for sale, absorption by the centre, or extinction (Lopreato, 2002). The total obtained through these privatisations was US$34.7 billion.

Another indication that the relative power of centre and states had shifted occurred in 1999. In January of that year, the new governor of Minas Gerais defaulted on the debt workout agreement signed by his predecessor. In response the President retained federal transfers of shared taxes from the Minas government while he manoeuvred patronage to ensure that other states would not also default.[3]

In addition to the shift in the power of centre and states, another important shift occurred in the executive–legislature relationship. According to the 1988 Constitution, principal responsibility for setting state debt limits, debt service caps, and approval of new loans fell to the Senate. In particular, the Economic Affairs Committee evaluated, and generally approved, sub-national requests for new debt and debt service levels. The reason approval was so forthcoming was that members of this committee used their position to support allies in state government or to promote their own election to executive positions in the states in subsequent years. The Senate was only neutralised when evidence emerged in 1997 that the Senate, with grudging Central Bank approval, had been approving state and municipal bonds issued to cover sub-national court obligations. These bonds were issued with inflated values, and, worse, they were marketed through a series of poorly regulated brokerage houses at large discounts. As the bonds exchanged hands, the gains realised from the discounts were skimmed off and laundered, some even finding their way into campaign coffers. As in other cases of scandal, nobody important was ever brought to justice, but it at least forced the Senate to restrain its generosity towards state indebtedness.

To institutionalise this restraint, Senate Law 78 in 1998 handed first-mover power to the Ministry of Finance in evaluating requests for sub-national debt. Instead of exerting political pressure to secure positive evaluations, senators now largely accept the positive or negative evaluation of creditworthiness provided by the Ministry of Finance (Webb, 2004). The new law prohibited loans to states holding primary deficits, reduced admissible levels of debt, and set a trajectory for gradual reduction of debt/revenue ratios (Rezende & Afonso, 2002: 16).

An additional shift was evident in the changing preferences of state leaders themselves (Cortez Reis, 2004). In his first term, Cardoso had spent political capital and patronage to secure an amendment to the Constitution that would allow re-election. In the context of renewed currency instability and the popularity of the Real Plan, Cardoso was re-elected in 1998, and on his coat-tails rode several governors; 21 of the 27 governors were members of his party or governing coalition. Most importantly, the key state of São Paulo was governed by a close Cardoso ally who shared his concern with renegotiating federal relations. The result was that most governors owed at least part of their political success to Cardoso, and many of them believed in his model of federalism reform.

As they entered power, many of these governors were looking for an excuse to implement the types of personnel cuts and privatisations that the central government demanded, and all they needed was a final push to allow incorporate these changes in a rearranged federalism.

The final push came shortly after the 1998 elections. A series of final shocks tilted the balance in favour of a wholesale change to federal institutions. Just prior to the elections, the Russian currency crisis shook world markets. Shortly thereafter, the Asian financial crisis suggested the possibility that numerous middle-income and emerging market economies could also be hit. Many considered Brazil to be due, partly because it had already weathered no fewer than seven crises since the mid-1980s, but also because the Real Plan had fixed a currency band that most observers knew to be overvalued. To get past the elections, Cardoso negotiated an agreement with the IMF but, less than a month after the beginning of the new government, the Minas default sparked a speculative crash that saw the currency fall by a third.

The crash was significant for several reasons, not least the disappearance of billions in Brazilian reserves and the apparent mismanagement of an exchange rate liberalisation. Brazilians, especially those close to the President, stressed the need to send firm signals to external creditors that the stabilisation regime would not be threatened. The signal was sent in the form of the Fiscal Responsibility Law. This law aggregated measures that were already on the books, repackaged them, and added more firm commitments (Tavares, 1999). In addition, it created new institutional mechanisms to manage the behaviour of different levels of government and the relationships between them. The moment and manner in which this reform was introduced was also strategic, occurring in the first year of Cardoso's new administration and packaged within the positive sounding title of 'responsibility'.

The law was presented to Congress in April 1999 after several months of consultations, including public consultation over the Internet. It passed through Special Committee in the Chamber of Deputies in December, passed the floor in January 2000, and was signed into law on 4th May. In parallel, though somewhat more slowly, a Fiscal Crimes Law was passed in October that year and established penalties for public officials who failed to comply with fiscal responsibility. These penalties included administrative, financial, and political penalties, and even prison time.

The law stipulated that limits would be established on public debt as a percentage of current receipts for the federal, state, and municipal levels. The limit for states has been set at two times current receipts, for municipalities 1.2 times, and discussions are under way for the federal government. If indebtedness levels exceed the ceilings, measures must be taken within 12 months to reduce the excess by at least 25 per cent within the first four months. Later, the Senate added a provision that states over the limit by the end of 2002 will have 15 years to adjust at 1/15 each year. The law also stipulates a golden rule for credit operations, that they cannot exceed capital expenses. In addition, the law specifically forbids bailouts of one level of government by another. Finally, the law controls one of the mechanisms of state finance that had been most abused prior to the debt workouts: the refinancing of loans in anticipation of receipts. Such anticipations have been forbidden entirely in electoral years (Rodden, 2003). Within the last year of a term, there is a further limit on new payment obligations unless administrations can demonstrate that the expenses can be fully paid within the term or there is sufficient cash for unpaid obligations in the next term.

The law also established rules for transparency in accounts. All levels of government have to publish fiscal targets for receipts, expenses, nominal balance, primary balance, public debt, and estimates of state enterprises, pension systems, and other obligations. These accounting and planning exercises are now codified and regulated according to standards set by the National Treasury and had to be published in the first phase of the budget process when the Budget Directives Laws were passed. There are also norms for consolidating and disseminating annual accounts and for producing quarterly reports on fiscal performance, published according to a common set of concepts and available on the internet.

The Fiscal Responsibility Law also established ceilings on personnel expenses. In 1995, the Camata Law had set a ceiling of personnel expenses equal to 50 per cent of current net revenue, and scheduled a timetable for states and municipalities to comply with that ceiling eventually, but most did not. The caps reappeared at 60 per cent of current revenues in the debt service agreements post-1997, but even these levels were not obeyed. It was only with the specific ceilings of the Fiscal Responsibility Law that personnel expenses began to fall. At federal level, the maximum limit is 50 per cent of current net revenue, while at the state and municipal levels it is 60 per cent. Each branch of government has its own ceilings also. The executive branch at the federal level is allowed 37 per cent, legislative 2.5 per cent, judiciary 6 per cent, and Attorney General 0.6 per cent. At the state level the percentages are 49 per cent, 3 per cent, 6 per cent, and 2 per cent respectively, and at the municipal level 54 per cent executive and 6 per cent for city councils.

In the case of a level of government or a branch of government failing to meet personnel targets, the law stipulates a pattern of transition, and contains sanctions that include retention of federal transfers and administrative penalties. If 95 per cent of the maximum limit for personnel is exceeded, the granting of new benefits to revenue officers, the creation of offices and new admissions, and overtime will be suspended. Also, if officials fail to implement, collect and charge levies under their jurisdiction, voluntary transfers to their jurisdiction will be suspended. With regard to personal sanctions, officials may be removed from office, prevented from occupying public posts, forced to pay fines, and serve prison sentences (Tavares, 2001; Serra & Afonso, 2002). The result has been a rapid decline in personnel expenses from 65 per cent of state revenues in 1999 to 54 per cent by 2002 (Alston *et al.*, 2004: 73).

These personnel limits attracted some civil society and partisan opposition. Public sector workers, sensing a threat, mobilised, and their chief partisan ally, the Workers' Party, articulated their concerns. Yet, several factors made this civil society and partisan opposition weak. First, the public sector most able to influence Congressional proceedings was at the federal level. Administrative reform there had preceded the Fiscal Responsibility Law and the new law would not imply additional cuts (interview with legislative aide). As a result, federal public workers were not easy to mobilise to defend workers at sub-national levels, and there was only limited pressure during Congressional proceedings.

The partisan opposition of the Workers' Party was also relatively ineffective. For one thing, many party members agreed with basic tenets of fiscal responsibility, and most of their executives at sub-national government were already well within limits stipulated by the law. There were elements of opposition to what was branded an 'IMF-style' or 'externally driven' piece of legislation (Bruno, 2000: 111–113), but this opposition was really only lukewarm. It was easily overcome by the rapporteur of the Special Commission, Pedro Novais, who had been specifically chosen to use his position to limit the number of amendments. Of 110 amendments presented, Novais accepted only 30, and it was passed with a simple majority (Bruno, 2000: 386–387).

Analysis of the federal system since the passage of the Fiscal Responsibility Law suggests a number of important changes under way. Between 2000 and 2002, 18 states improved their personnel/revenue ratio and only three states were above the limits set by the law (see Table 1). Debt ratios also improved in 16 out of the 27 states. By 2002, only seven remained above the debt ceilings set by the Senate. In the same period, 18 states also improved their primary surpluses, eight went from deficits to surpluses and only three presented primary deficits in 2002 (Nunes & Nunes, 2003).

The Fiscal Responsibility Law of 2000 in Brazil can be viewed from several perspectives. To some of those involved, it was the bold move of a group of enlightened Brazilian politicians that had finally put their federal house in order:

> The approval of the law reflects the extraordinary change in parliamentary behaviour . . .. Not only did the Congress approve the law, but an overwhelming majority of authorities and legislators from states and municipalities understood that she represented a decisive step for the federal republic, almost one century after its initiation, to achieve its potential . . .. This profound movement of the fiscal pattern in Brazil has been recognised internationally . . . and the IMF concluded that it was a watershed event. (Serra & Afonso, 2002: 4–5)

To others, the law was simply the next step in a path-dependent trajectory that could potentially be reversed:

> The principal conclusion of this project is that the Law does not represent a point of rupture. The more likely scenario is that the law

represents only one more link, though an important one, in a chain of events that are frequently ambiguous and not rarely contradictory, in the federal history of Brazil. In this sense, from the point of view of broadly evaluating the paths of stability or change in institutions, it can be said that the Law is no more and no less vulnerable to political conjunctures as past institutional arrangements. (Guimarães, 2004: 138)

Table 1. Consolidated debt and personnel as a percentage of liquid receipts

	Debt				Personnel/receipts (%)			
	2000	2001	2002	2003	2000	2001	2002	2003
Average per cent current liquid receipts	1.70	1.73	1.94	1.79	47.85	45.97	45.49	45.32
No. of states above the legal limits	7	5	8	8	7	2	3	3

Source: National Treasury Secretary.

The current project takes a middle road. The Fiscal Responsibility Law in Brazil marked the passage of a threshold. Brazilian federalism is indeed different than it was before, most particularly because sub-national governments must now obey a relatively hard budget constraint. Still, this threshold was not passed in a sudden leap. Rather, subtle shifts and adjustments in the preferences of different actors, their relative power, and the institutions in which they operated meant that the federal pact of 1988 had been surpassed. Beginning in 1994, a number of legislative and institutional steps moved towards a new pact, and the Fiscal Responsibility Law represented the culmination of the long process of forming a new federal arrangement.

Within-Institution Change: The Fiscal Pact Around Tax

Like the pact supporting federalism after 1988, the pact around tax appeared intractable before the 1990s. It was. A major tax reform had occurred under the military regime in 1967, and even the 1988 Constitutional Convention failed to establish a new consensus on who should pay what to which level of government. During the 1990s, fiscal crisis put tax back on the agenda, but no wholesale change was to occur. Instead, the existing pact was modified around the edges, and change occurred within the boundaries of previous arrangements. This does not mean that nothing happened; tax capacity increased by over 10 per cent of GDP, and there were also notable improvements in the administration and rationality of certain taxes, such as income tax. Still, the changes failed to support more significant change, and the increase in the tax burden came at the cost of economic inefficiency and continued inequality (Werneck, 2000; Varsano, 2003).

This is the key to summarising the tax reform as an increase in capacity without an increase in accountability. Instead of forging a new pact around tax, all actors manoeuvred within the boundaries of previous tax institutions to face challenges as they emerged. They were able to use administrative and legal tools to mobilise greater resources, but they could not forge a new pact around the issue of tax. As a result, there was no ability to include new actors, redefine state–society relations, or, more generally, increase government accountability around the issue of tax. Had they been able to do so, they would not only have increased the revenues available through tax, they would also have been able to address the inefficiency and inequality of the Brazilian tax system. From the earliest days of reform, Deputy Marcos Cintra noted acidly, 'The reform project of the government was a deception. In reality, it has been only a bandaid' (*Folha de São Paulo*, 1995).

The architecture of current Brazilian tax institutions was largely set under the military in the 1967 Constitution (Varsano, 1996, 2003). The code gave central government the authority to define sub-national tax rates and exemptions, lowered the portion of federal taxes to be shared with states, and reserved the power to establish social contributions to the federal level (Lopreato, 2002: 26).

Income tax had been under discussion since even before the military came to power, and it was reformed to shift burdens and expand collection. What most characterised the system was its repeated use to direct and stimulate capital accumulation through incentives for particular groups and sectors, and the result has been increased inequality and heavy burdens on formal sector labour (Varsano, 2003).

Additional reforms included replacing a series of cascading sales taxes with a tax on goods and services that made Brazil a pioneer in the use of value added tax (VAT). Cascading taxes pass the cost of taxes through to consumers, such that consumers end up paying tax not only on the value of products they buy but also on the value of taxes paid at each stage of production. Eliminating these cascading effects was a vast improvement but, unlike later versions of VAT popular around the world, the Brazilian tax was complicated by variation within the country. Different rates were applied to different goods and both state and national level had their own sales taxes. In addition, the Brazilian version is based on the restricted origin principle, which potentially favours states that are net exporters of taxed goods, and, in response to pressure from poorer states, a lower tax was applied to cross-border trade and importing and exporting states share the revenues of goods crossing borders.

The problem is that over time the sales tax system has become even more complex than the income tax system. In economic terms, this complexity damages efficiency by introducing distortions and fiscal outcomes by facilitating evasion. In administrative terms, complexity makes even more difficult the task of collection. In distributional terms, complexity is regressive, as the wealthy are more able to escape tax or use their influence to seek benefits. Finally, in the political economic terms being applied here, complexity has made it even more difficult to introduce reform, as each beneficiary of an exemption or incentive under the current system resists change, even if it is likely to be to their benefit, because of uncertainties over outcomes (Fernandez & Rodrik, 1991; Varsano, 2003).

The system established by the military also created distortions as a result of its manipulation of decentralisation to sustain its power. At the peak of centralisation, constitutional transfers were just 5 per cent of income tax and the tax on industrial products. In attempts to retain power during the 1970s, the central government increased transfers, and by 1988 they reached 14 per cent for states and 17 per cent for municipalities (Medeiros, 1986). Over time, transfers became more and more untied, providing lower levels with block grants to allocate largely as they wished (Serra & Afonso, 2002).

Combined with the incentives granted to different sectors, this meant that the central government was losing revenues. To sustain tax capacity at approximately 25 per cent of GDP, the regime imposed a number of social contributions that were collected into funds and not shared with other levels of government. Once again, the burden of contributions fell on the formal sector, increasing the cost of labour without increasing wages or contributing to productivity.

The structure of revenues that the military left to the democratic regime was characterised by complexity, regressivity, and distortion, though administrative capacity had been established and the state was able to secure significant resources. The fiscal crises of the 1980s and 1990s meant that even more revenues would be necessary, and there was a broad demand to address the other problems of the system, which weighed heavily on the most productive sectors. Attempts to increase revenues succeeded, but attempts to raise revenues in a more efficient and equitable fashion failed.

The first real attempt occurred at the Constitutional Convention of 1988. In the context of redesigning Brazilian democracy, everything was on the table, including tax. Yet, the discussions were distracted by localist and regional pressures, and instead of dealing with basic questions of equity and efficiency, the debate focused on reorganising the federal dimensions of the tax system (Souza, 1997). 'The distribution of tax revenue among units of the three levels of government was the main issue. The backbone of the tax system remained practically intact' (Varsano, 2003: 4).

The Constitution fixed high levels of block grant transfers to sub-national units (44 per cent of income tax and industrial goods tax) and confirmed the autonomy of states and municipalities to control their own tax bases. The state sales tax on goods was expanded to areas (such as fuel, energy, telecommunications, transport and minerals) that had previously rested with central government, and municipalities were given control over sales taxes on services. Central government retained several exclusive taxes, including social contributions.

The result was actually worse than what existed before. The revenue scheme exacerbated inequality across states, with the ratio between the states with highest and lowest tax capacity at 9.4 (Prado, 2001: 50). Also, though the federal transfer system includes a progressive formula to address some of these inequalities (Rezende & Afonso, 2002: 115), there is nothing in place to address inequalities across municipalities in individual states (Prado, 2001: 54). In fact, some of the least progressive internal distributions of tax capacity are in the poor north-eastern states that receive the most transfers from the federal government. Further, negotiated transfers worked against the progressive formula for constitutional transfers; wealthier states tended to benefit disproportionately. These negotiated transfers almost doubled from 1995 to 2000, and most were directed towards states that were politically important to coalition-building at the federal level (Rodden & Arretche, 2004).

It should be noted that pressure from civil society, progressive political elites, and the general mood of democratisation turned some attention to equity issues. A tax on wealth was created, and the federal government reaffirmed its role taxing rural property. Unfortunately, these measures neither provided significant revenues nor were implemented to any significant degree. In fact, the tax on large fortunes remains unregulated (Varsano, 2003; interview, Everardo Maciel).

Other attempts to reform the tax system followed and produced similarly dismal results. In 1991, facing fiscal and currency crisis, President Collor pursued a reform labelled the Big Amendment (Emendão). This included emergency measures that set top personal income tax rates at 35 per cent and introduced a tax on financial transactions. For a time, it secured an increase in tax capacity that raised taxation levels close to 30 per cent of GDP. Yet Collor had failed to build a real pact around these issues, and had largely made use of autocratic powers left to the executive from the military regime (Castro Santos *et al.*, 1994). He proved unable to build a parliamentary coalition, and taxes soon dropped to their previous level. In fact, parliament soon tired of his high-handed strategies and, in the midst of a corruption scandal, Collor was eventually impeached.

Following the Real Plan, attempts at a global reform were reinitiated in 1997, this time spearheaded by a special committee in Congress. Acting with the support of the industrial and financial sectors, the Special Committee generated a reform proposal that targeted both sales taxes and contributions (interview, President of the National Confederation of Industries). The proposal included broad consultations with political parties, state governments, the private sector, and the federal executive, and a proposal was launched in 1999.

The heart of the reform addressed the sales tax. The state sales tax (ICMS) continues to be the most important tax in terms of collection, and it accounts for approximately 30 per cent of all taxes collected (Varsano *et al.*, 1998; Prado, 2001). Yet, the tax remains complex, with an average rate of 18 per cent, but different rates across states, 44 different categories for goods, and the origin principle on goods in which exporting and importing states must split revenues.

The reform sought to eliminate some of this complexity, but it was blocked by uncertainty, made worse in the context of fiscal crisis. One observer from the Ministry of Finance agrees: 'It is not that the states or some group of states are too powerful, it is that neither the states nor the federal government want to run the risk of losing money.' Given this context of uncertainty, multiple actors found ways of derailing the process. The rapporteur in the Special Committee, Mussa Demes, had been a state secretary of finance, and he committed himself to protecting the revenues of the states. The central government responded with its own attacks: 'The reform presented by Mussa Demes has a series of loopholes favouring, above all, evangelical legislators with links to radio stations, and industries in the Manaus free trade zone', and there was almost no progress (*Correio Braziliense*, 1999).

Given the failure to undertake wholesale reform, changes were limited to those possible within the boundaries of the already existing tax structure. The first change was triggered by the Real Plan of 1994. The plan depended on a fiscal adjustment, and cutting spending was, and continues to be, exceedingly difficult. Instead, the central government sought to increase taxes and reduce the portion of revenues shared with the sub-national level. A constitutional amendment retained 20 per cent of earmarked tax revenues in a distractingly labelled 'Social Emergency Fund' (FSE). To acquire the two-thirds majority needed for the amendment, the president who replaced Collor, Itamar Franco, had to enter into complicated bargaining with the Chamber and the Senate, and had to agree to a time limit on the fund. In ensuing years, each time the limit was set to expire, the central government renewed the fund under different names (Fiscal Stabilisation Fund, Disconnection of Union Revenues), and used logrolling and patronage within the legislature to secure an extension.

The federal government recuperated some of the ground it had lost to the states and municipalities. From 1983 to 1995, the federal government had lost progressively more ground through growing constitutional transfers. Central revenues as a percentage of the total were 69.1 per cent in 1983, and fell to 56.2 per cent in 1995. From 1995 to 2000 the trend reversed, however, and central revenue increased to 59.9 per cent (Samuels, 2003: 555–556).

The federal government also expanded its share through the use of contributions (see Table 2). Contributions were attractive because they came into effect three months after initiation (instead of the following year, as with normal taxes); they were not shared sub-nationally; they required only a simple majority to approve (not a supermajority and special congressional committee); and their costs were spread across the entire productive sector yet were virtually invisible automatic deductions and withholdings (Lledo, 2005).

Among the nine major contributions, five were payroll taxes dedicated to pensions and other benefit systems. Originally, the contribution on financial transactions was passed as a temporary measure by Collor and was subsequently declared unconstitutional. A political bargain to patch up a health crisis in 1996 brought the tax back, but only on a temporary basis (Piola & Biasoto, 2001). The contribution was renewed in 1998, unconnected to health, and it has survived as a repeatedly renewed temporary measure. As a proportion of total revenues, contributions climbed from 27.2 per cent to 46.7 per cent between 1990 and 2001 (Samuels, 2003: 556; see also Rezende *et al.*, 2002). In total, contributions accounted for approximately half of the growth in tax as a percentage of GDP during the 1990s (Afonso, 2000).

The marginal successes that were observed over the period are testament to both the importance of pacts for making change, and their difficulty. Three of these successes will be examined here: exports, income, and cascades. In 1995, the Kandir Law (part of Proposta de Emenda Constitucional (PEC) 175/95), exempted international exports from state sales taxes, and thus

Table 2. Tax burden and distribution across levels of government

Year	Tax burden (% of GDP)	Share in total tax collected (%)			Share in disposable revenue (%)		
		Union	States	Local	Union	States	Local
1960	17.41	64.0	31.3	4.7	59.5	34.1	6.4
1970	25.98	66.7	30.6	2.7	60.8	29.2	10.0
1983	26.97	76.5	20.6	2.8	69.8	21.3	8.9
1988	22.43	71.7	25.6	2.7	60.1	26.6	13.3
1995	29.41	66.0	28.6	5.4	56.2	27.2	16.6
2001	34.36	68.7	26.8	4.5	59.3	26.5	14.2

Source: Varsano (2003).

removed a major obstacle to Brazil's continued liberalisation. It was possible through a side-payment, in which the chief architect of the law, Deputy Antonio Kandir, negotiated with different states to establish a compensation fund for lost revenues. Agricultural exporting states formed the most significant lobby, and they secured favourable terms, though they have been unable to hold the federal government to its promises.

A more significant change was made in income tax. Brazil followed international trends and dropped its income tax and profit contributions to approximately 25 per cent for the top marginal bracket (Ministerio de Fazenda, 2001: 108–110). Through temporary measures the top bracket was raised to 27.5 per cent. Like the withholding of sub-national transfers, tax increases presented as temporary were an easier pill for legislators to swallow. Income tax over the period increased by over 50 per cent, and increased as a portion of total taxes from 13.8 per cent in 1994 to 16.7 per cent in 2000.

In addition, income tax reforms also simplified administration and compliance. Incentives were eliminated, and rates were unified across different sources of personal, corporate, and financial income. For small and medium-sized businesses, new forms of simplified tax (SIMPLES for small business and Presumed Income for medium businesses) replaced a series of contributions and taxes that were difficult and costly to administer. In 1999, firms paying the SIMPLES and Presumed Income taxes accounted for over 16 per cent of corporate income tax and included over 92 per cent of all registered firms.

Most of these changes were possible through bureaucratic decree, and those that had to be approved by Congress required only a simple majority. The general strategy was to leave the debate over tax until the end of the year, and Congressional discussions of pet expenditure projects were held hostage to passing tax increases.

The most significant income tax gains were made in the financial sector. By redefining and equalising the rates for different forms of financial assets and income and extending the concepts of profit and employment contributions to the financial sector, government was able to net almost R$2.4 billion in 2000 alone (Ministerio de Fazenda, 2001: 135). Everardo Maciel, Secretary of the Tax Administration at the time, explained the success of the reform in terms of strategies pursued following the Real Plan, when the most powerful banking interests faced outstanding judicial cases as a result of rapid changes in inflation and interest rates. As Maciel explained, 'I resolved the judicial cases outstanding, and in the process, left the adversary weak. Afterwards, I negotiated with FEBRABAM [the Association of Banks] over taxes on the financial sector. The difference was R$22 billion to federal revenues.' Greatly softening the blow to the financial sector were the high interest rates associated with the Real Plan. In effect, Maciel could engage in hard-nosed bargaining to extract revenues because the banks knew they would recoup any payments though interest rates that rose above 40 per cent and holding government debt, which exploded during the period.

Finally, there were some steps towards eliminating the most damaging cascading effects of contributions. Because contributions are paid as a value of labour used, the cost is passed from one stage of production to the next, raising the price of products, and ultimately being passed to the consumer. Using presidential decree powers, the executive proposed a change to the contributions that would replace a cascading 3 per cent rate with a non-cascading 7 per cent rate. The new rate was meant to be revenue neutral, though the executive simply delayed presenting the evidence of revenue neutrality until after Congress had to vote on the bill. To get the law through, once again a series of side-payments was necessary. Subcategories of the private sector, such as transport and agriculture, argued that shorter production chains should be allowed to retain the prior cascading 3 per cent rate in place of the non-cascading 7 per cent.

There were important triumphs in changing the tax regime during the 1990s and early 2000s: the modernisation of the income tax regime, the exemption of exports from sales tax, the elimination of some elements of cascading contributions, and the extremely impressive increase in tax capacity. Yet, even these reforms were achieved under the radar of important political actors. There was little public discussion of the changes that actually occurred, and no new pact around tax led to their approval.

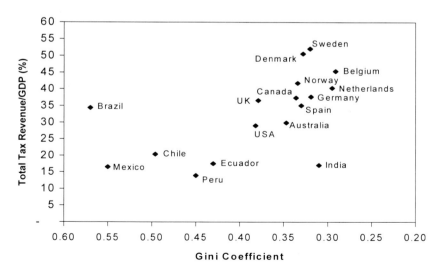

Figure 1. Tax burden and gini coefficient. *Source:* Bezerra de Siqueira *et al.* (2003: 5)

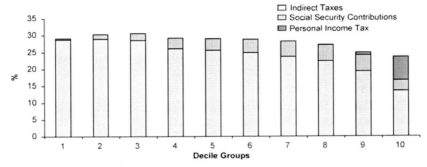

Figure 2. Taxes as a proportion of household gross income by decile group. *Source*: Bezerra de Siqueira *et al.* (2003: 11)

The reforms passed unnoticed by the population in general and even among specialists because they were done gradually, in the context of a well-structured project that required only ordinary legislation to promote. For that reason, it was not necessary to confront the conflicts and difficulties typical of constitutional tax reform (Ministerio da Fazenda, 2001: 137).

The failure to engage in a new social pact around tax has preserved some of its worst characteristics, in particular its inequity. As many have noted, Brazil is the single most unequal country in the world. One might expect a country that mobilises so many resources to combat inequality effectively; yet, Brazilian inequality remains far worse than other countries that tax at similar levels (Bezerra de Siqueira *et al.*, 2003). In fact, Brazil is an obvious outlier in a graph that plots tax burden and gini coefficient (Figure 1). Most countries with levels of inequality comparable to Brazil tax far less, and most countries that tax heavily do a much better job of redistribution.

When one considers the proportion of household income that Brazilians pay in tax, poor households end up contributing more. Direct taxes practically hit only the highest income brackets, and the poorest households (mainly in the informal sector) largely escape social contributions. Still, if one assumes that producers shift social contributions to consumers, the incidence of taxes almost uniformly decreases with income. Figure 2 displays the proportion of household income paid in tax by different deciles of the population. The richest deciles pay more direct taxes, as would be expected, but they still pay less of their income in tax.

Conclusion

One cannot help but wonder why a new pact around the Fiscal Responsibility Law was possible, while it was impossible for tax. Both reforms represent governance changes and, in this sense, they shared some similarities. They were both gradual and incremental processes in which interests, power, and inherited institutions mattered. What set the two reform processes apart was whether incremental changes in these variables built towards a new pact or not.

The incremental process leading to the Fiscal Responsibility Law served to weaken opponents, strengthen supporters, and adjust institutions in ways that directed actors' interests towards reform. In particular, the principal opponents of reform found their positions weakened and shifted over the course of the decade. Ultimately, this reached a threshold that the Fiscal Responsibility Law was able to breach. The law was the result of a new pact around public finances and federal relations.

In the case of tax, incremental changes occurred within existing institutions and did not accumulate to a new pact around tax. Explicit attempts to forge a pact among social, political, and federal actors were unsuccessful, and actors remained content to operate within the boundaries of inherited institutions. This meant that certain perversions continued and were exacerbated. The federal government made use of decree power and institutional rules to raise revenues, but it did so by using cascading contributions and retaining transfers it was meant to share. States made use of the autonomy they had gained in the 1988 Constitution to engage in fiscal competition over the sales tax, and the result was an inefficient tax system that raised significant revenues but carried an economic cost in distortions, disincentives, and inequities. The few episodes of reform that occurred were limited to the boundaries of existing institutions, and did not seriously upset or threaten existing pacts.

The role of fiscal crisis is interesting in both cases. In the case of the Fiscal Responsibility Law, the crisis of 1999 offered the final push to tip the balance in favour of reform. In the case of tax reform, fiscal crisis did not overcome the coordination and uncertainty problems involved in creating a new pact, and may even have complicated matters. When it came to taxes, crisis made all actors more insecure about losing revenues, and the central government in particular was unwilling to push for reform.

A few other observations are relevant. Much of the preceding discussion has focused on the Machiavellian 'high' politics of manoeuvres and manipulations to disarm opponents and strengthen allies. Indeed, this is the stuff of everyday politics in which contingency and agency are crucially important. Machiavellian manoeuvres were sufficient to bring about wholesale change in Brazilian federalism, but the same kind of politics was only sufficient for within-institution change in the case of tax.

The reason high politics was sufficient in one case and not in another may lie in the nature of social actors that had to be coordinated. In the case of federalism, there were fierce opponents to reform but these were mostly located among the political elite (senators, governors, bureaucrats). These actors were drawn from a narrow group, and could be co-opted, cajoled, or coerced into cooperation.

By contrast, wholesale change in tax institutions would have required a much more fundamental and structural renegotiation. The same political elite was at the centre of the process, but it operated as representative of wider social and economic interests. Governors opposing the reforms acted as members of different regions, and they saw tax as a struggle between fundamentally opposed interests such as domestic/external orientation, agriculture/industry, labour/ capital. There were fewer possibilities of coalitions when the interests in opposition were deeply rooted. Instead of facing up to the task of a new pact, tax reform focused on the high politics of intra-elite negotiation, side-payments, and avoiding conflict. This was sufficient to achieve within-institution change, but it could never approach wholesale change.

In closing, it is appropriate to strike a somewhat lighter tone. The governance impacts of federal reform and tax reform are infinite improvements over patterns that existed previously. Both reforms increased the capacity of the state while moving towards more modern patterns of operation. That said, wholesale change in federalism was more significant for two reasons. First, the Fiscal Responsibility Law created new institutions; tax reform only involved adjustment at the margins of existing institutions. Second, the process of achieving wholesale change depended on the construction of a social new pact. In relation to tax, this was not possible, and one has to question the durability of the marginal gains made to date.

Notes

1. The notion of necessary and sufficient causes was usefully raised by Poul Engberg-Pedersen and has been discussed extensively by Goetz and Starr (2002).
2. Selene Nunes, one of the architects of the legislation, has made this extremely clear in personal communication and in several of her published evaluations (Nunes & Nunes, 2003).
3. The hard line taken with Minas was no coincidence. The governor of Minas, Itamar Franco, had been president from 1993 to 1994 and was a political rival to President Fernando Henrique Cardoso. The Minas default was Itamar's calculated move to test the resolve of both president and opposition. Unfortunately for Itamar, he had not calculated the political winds particularly well. Though a few other opposition governors threatened defaults of their own, they soon resumed payments with much less fanfare, and governors failed to support a collective renegotiation (Samuels, 2003: 554).

References

Afonso, J. R. (2000) *Brazil: Fiscal Federalism, Tax Modernization, and Consumption and Production Taxes* (São Paulo: SF/BNDES).

Alston, L. J., Melo, M. A., Mueller, B. & Pereira, C. (2004) *Political Institutions, Policymaking Processes and Policy Outcomes in Brazil* (Brasilia: Inter-American Development Bank).

Bezerra de Siqueira, R., Nogueira, J. R., Levy, H., Immervoll, H. & O'Donoghue, C. (2003) *The Redistributive Effects of the Brazilian Tax–Benefit System: A Micro-simulation Analysis* (Brasilia: Ibero-America Institute for Economic Research).

Bruno, R. M. (2000) *Lei de Responsibilidade Fiscal e Orcamento Publico Municipal* (São Paulo: Editora Afiliada).

Campos, J. E. & Pradhan, S. (2003) A *Framework for Studying Governance. Reforms at the Country Level*, unpublished mimeo (Washington, DC: World Bank).

Castro Santos, M. H. de, Gracas Rua, M. das, Massimo Machado, E. & Peixoto Machado, A. L. B. (1994) Interesses Sociais e Poderes Constituidos na Politica Fiscal e Tributaria dos Governos Collor e Itamar Franco: Padroes de Interacao, Conflitos, e Barganhas, *Caderno de Ciencia Politica*, 11.

Collier, D. & Collier, R. B. (1991) *Shaping the Political Arena: Critical Junctures, The Labor Movement, and Regime Dynamics in Latin America* (Princeton, NJ: Princeton University Press).

Correio Braziliense (1999), 27 November.

Cortez Reis, M. (2004) Os *Efeitos da Performance Econômica e de Políticas Fiscais Sobre os Resultados Eleitorais: Evidências das Eleições para Governador no Brasil*, mimeo, Brasília.

Dillinger, W. (1995) *Brazil State Debt: Crisis and Reform* (Washington, DC: World Bank).

Dillinger, W. & Webb, S. (1999) *Fiscal Management in Federal Democracies: Argentina and Brazil* (Washington, DC: World Bank Group).

Fernandez, R. & Rodrik, D. (1991) Resistance to reform: status quo bias in the presence of individual-specific uncertainty, *American Economic Association*, 81(5), pp. 1146–1155.

Folha de São Paulo (1995), 26 November.

Giambiagi, F. & Além, A. C. (2001) *Financas Públicas: Teoria e Práctica no Brasil 2nda edição* (Rio de Janeiro: Editora Campus).

Goertz, G. & Starr, H. (Eds) (2002) *Necessary Conditions: Theory, Methodology, and Applications* (New York: Rowman & Littlefield).

Goldfajn, I. & Guardia, E. R. (2003) Regras Fiscais e Sustentabilidade da Divida no Brasil, *Notas Tecnicas do Banco Central do Brasil*, 39 (Julho), pp. 1–27.

Guimarães, H. (2004) *Instituicoes e Federalismo Fiscal no Brasil: Um Estudo do Caso da Lei de Responsibilidade Fiscal* (Mestrado: Instituto de Ciencia Politica, UnB, Brasilia).

Huntington, S. P. (1968) *Political Order in Changing Societies* (New Haven, CT: Yale University Press).

International Monetary Fund (2001) *Brazil: Report on Observance of Standards and Codes* (Rosc) – Fiscal Transparency, IMF Country Report 01/217 (Washington, DC: IMF).

Lledo, V. D. (2005) *Tax Systems Under Fiscal Adjustment: A Dynamic CGE Analysis of the Brazilian Tax Reform*, IMF Working Paper (Washington, DC: IMF).

Lopreato, F. L. C. (2002) *O Colapso das Financas Estaduais e a Crise da Federacao* (São Paulo: Instituto de Economia).

Mahoney, J. (2000) Path dependence in historical sociology, *Theory and Society*, 29(4), (August), pp. 507–548.

Medeiros, A. C. (1986) *Intergovernmental Relations in Brazil 1964–1982*, Doctoral Dissertation, London School of Economics (London: Frances Pinter).

Ministerio da Fazenda (2001) *Carga Tributaria No Brasil* (Secretaria de Receita, Federal, Coordenacao General de Politica Tributaria, Brasil).

Mora, M. & Varsano, R. (2001) *Fiscal Decentralization and Sub-national Fiscal Autonomy in Brazil: Some Facts of the Nineties*, Discussion Paper 854, IPEA, mimeo, Rio de Janeiro.

North, D. C. (1991) *Institutions, Institutional Change and Economic Performance* (New York: Cambridge University Press).

Nunes, S. P. & Nunes, R da C. (2003) *Dois Anos da Lei de Responsabilidade Fiscal do Brasil: Uma Avaliacao dos Resultados a Luz do Modelo do Fundo Comum* (Brasilia: Departamento de Economia – UnB)

Perry, G. & Webb, S. (1999) Addressing the macroeconomic threat: the quest for hard budget constraints, in: S. Burki (Ed.) *Beyond the Center: Decentralizing the State* (Washington, DC: World Bank).

Piola, S. F. & Biasoto, G. Jr (2001) Financiamento do SUS nos Anos 90, in: B. Negri & G. Giovanni, *Radiográfia da Saude* (Campinas: Instituto de Economia), pp. 219–32.

Pierson, P. (2000) Path dependence, increasing returns, and the study of politics, *American Political Science Review*, 94(2), pp. 251–267.

Prado, S. (2001) *Transferencias Fiscais e Financiamento Municipal no Brasil* (São Paulo: EBAP/Fundacao Konrad Adenaur).

Rezende, F. & Afonso, J. R. (2002) *The Brazilian Federation: Facts, Challenges, and Prospects* (Stanford, CA: Stanford University Press).

Rezende, S., Antonio, F. & Cunha, M. (2002) *Contribuintes e Cidadãos: Compreendendo o Orçamento Federal* (Rio de Janeiro: Editora FGV).

Rodden, J. (2003) Federalism and bailouts in Brazil, in: J. Rodden, G. Eskeland & J. Litvack (Eds) *Fiscal Decentralization and the Challenge of Hard Budget Constraints* (Cambridge, MA: MIT Press).

Rodden, J. & Arretche, M. (2004) Legislative Bargaining and Distributive Politics in Brazil: An Empirical Approach, unpublished paper, MIT Press, Cambridge, MA.

Rodden, J., Eskeland, G. & Litvack, J. (Eds) (2003) *Fiscal Decentralization and the Challenge of Hard Budget Constraints* (Cambridge, MA: MIT Press).

Samuels, D. (2003) Fiscal straightjacket: the political economy of macroeconomic reform in Brazil, 1995–2002, *Journal of Latin American Studies*, 35(3), pp. 545–569.

Serra, J. & Afonso, J. R (2002) *Fiscal Federalism Brazilian Style: Reflections*, Available at http://www.federativo.bndes.gov.br/bf_bancos/estudos/e0001792.pdf: BNDES.

Souza, C. (1997) *Constitutional Engineering in Brazil: The Politics of Federalism and Decentralization* (New York: St Martin's Press).

Stepan, A. (2000) Brazil's decentralized federalism: bringing government closer to the citizens?, *Daedalus*, spring, pp 145–169.

Tavares, M. (2001) *Fazendo o Dever de Casa com Responsibilidade*, Folha de São Paulo, May.

Tavares, M. (1999) Responsibilidade Fiscal y Competencia Politica, *O Globo*, April.

Ter-Minassian, T. (1997) *Fiscal Federalism: Theory and Practice* (Washington, DC: International Monetary Fund).

Thelen, K. (2003) How Institutions evolve: insights from comparative-historical analysis, in: J. Mahoney & D. Reuschemeyer (Eds) *Comparative Historical Analysis in the Social Sciences* (Cambridge: Cambridge University Press).

Varsano, R. (1996) *A Evolucao do Sistema Tributario Brasileiro ao Longo do Seculo: Anotacoes e Reflexoes Para Futuras Reformas* (Brasilia: IPEA).

Varsano, R. (2003) *Tax Reform in Brazil: The Long Process in Progress* (Rio de Janeiro: IPEA).

Varsano, R., Pessoa, E. de P., Costa da Silva, N. L., Afonso, J. R., Araujo, E. A. & Ramundo, J. C. M. (1998) *Uma Analise da Carga Tributaria do Brasil* (Brasilia: IPEA).

Webb, S. (2004) *Fiscal Responsibility Laws for Sub-national Discipline: Latin American Experience*, World Bank Working Paper Series 3309 (Washington, DC: World Bank).

Werneck, R. L. F. (2000) *Tax Reform in Brazil: Small Achievements and Great Challenges* (Rio de Janeiro: PUC-Rio).

State Capacity, Accountability and Economic Development in Africa

BRIAN LEVY

The view that governance and its reform are key to development effectiveness is held increasingly widely. However, the results of governance reform efforts have been very mixed. There is thus an urgent need to extract lessons of experience. Paralleling the comparative analyses of Brazil, India and Uganda reported elsewhere in this issue, a similar exercise was under way at the World Bank.

This paper has three principal goals. First, it summarises the empirical record of Africa's development performance over the past quarter of a century in a way that highlights the interactions between economic perform-ance and the quality of governance. Second, it highlights some emerging find-ings as to what has worked (and what has not) in specific interventions in Africa aimed at building public bureaucratic capability, and at strengthening the institutions that hold the bureaucracy accountable for performance. Third, it distils from the specific findings some broader propositions as to how state capacity and accountability might most effectively be built.

As will become evident, there are some striking commonalities in the results of the African analysis, and the comparative case studies of Brazil, India and Uganda. Both exercises conclude that governance reform cannot usefully be viewed as a narrowly technical exercise. To be effective, governance reform must take as its point of departure a careful assessment of the way in which country-specific formal and informal political and social institutions shape the incentives for decision-makers to initiate and sustain governance reforms. In many (but not all) countries, such an assessment may signal the need to set aside ambitious agendas in favour of more incremental approaches to governance reform.

Governance and Economic Performance: Some Empirical Patterns

Africa's Neo-patrimonial Downward Spiral

Upon independence many African countries were bequeathed governance structures with a strong shell of formal institutions, both political and bureaucratic. Often, however, these seemingly richly articulated formal institutions turned out to be rather hollow, reflecting a combination of colonial legacy and high-minded aspirations of independence. In reality, the ability of many states to structure (beyond a narrow urban segment) political interests in a way that was supportive of a developmental project was weak.

The short-run consequence (Migdal, 1988) was that the mode of governance shifted rapidly from a formal system of checks and balances to a de facto (and, in many countries, also in part *de jure*) system of rule that has been described by African scholars as 'neo-patrimonial' (Dia, 1996; Lewis, 1996). Through the 1970s and 1980s neo-patrimonialism seemed to provide a stable, if not especially dynamic, form of rule. In practice, though – and as the subsequent unfolding of events in country after country confirmed – slow-moving, but inexorable, forces of decay underlay the neo-patrimonial model.

One area of decay was in the bureaucracy. At independence most bureaucracies were governed by formal rules and initially subject to relatively slight informal pressure from political interests. With the rise of neo-patrimonial rule, the mode of governing bureaucracy shifted from the clarification, monitoring, and enforcement of formal rules to informal rules set without transparency, and sometimes increasingly capriciously, by a country's political leadership. The consequence was a decline in bureaucratic performance.

The decline of bureaucracy influenced economic performance by affecting policy-making, regulation, and service delivery. Neo-patrimonial rule generally operated by conferring discretionary rents on favoured allies, giving little attention to the impact of rentier policies on economic growth, the efficiency of public services, or the quality of business regulation. The classic consequences, evident in country after country, included the disruption of markets, rising costs of doing business, urban bias, and increased protectionism.

The intensification of a rentier relationship between business and government progressively transformed the structure of the business class itself, bringing about a progressive rise of a politically dependent business class.

In some countries (Sierra Leone, for example) the neo-patrimonial downward spiral proceeded to the point of state collapse. In others domestic political intervention pre-empted the cycle of decline.

Adjustment and Economic Performance

Reversal of the neo-patrimonial downward spiral began in a small number of African countries in the mid-1980s and accelerated into the 1990s. The two most familiar facets of this reversal are structural adjustment economic reforms and the wave of democratisation that swept the continent in the early 1990s. The trajectories of adjustment and democratisation have been documented extensively elsewhere (Bratton and Van de Walle, 1997; World Bank, 1994). This section simply provides a summary overview of the economic impact of adjustment on a set of 21 African countries.[1]

The 21 countries can be grouped according to the degree to which the process of economic reform has been sustained and longstanding. Three groups are identified.

- The first group comprises the *sustained adjusters* – eight countries that consistently remained on track in their programmes of reform throughout the 1988–1996 rounds of financial support provided through the multi-donor Special Program for Africa. These countries are Benin, Burkina Faso, Ghana, Malawi, Mali, Mozambique, Uganda, and Zambia.
- The second group comprises eight *later adjusters* – countries that initiated strong policy reforms in the 1990s and continued to sustain their reforms to the end of 2001. These countries are Cameroon, Chad, Guinea, Madagascar, Mauritania, Niger, Senegal, and Tanzania.
- The third group comprises five *governance polarised* countries – Côte d'Ivoire, Kenya, Nigeria, Togo, and Zimbabwe. Although all of these countries initiated some policy reforms during the 1990s, in all cases domestic political disruptions of one kind or another overshadowed efforts at economic policy reform.

Table 1 reports the average annual real growth rates in GDP for these three groups of countries over four distinct periods.[2] Overall the sustained adjusters' commitment to policy reform since the late 1980s appears to have paid off, because growth accelerated in each period. Among the later adjusters, the overall pattern is one of slow growth prior to policy reform and subsequent acceleration. As for the last group, the contrast with the others is clear – the

Table 1. Average annual growth in real GDP for 21 African countries, 1975–2000

Country	1975–84	1985–89	1991–96	1996–2000
Eight sustained adjusters	1.7%	3.2%	3.7%	4.7%
Eight later adjusters	2.4%	2.7%	1.9%	4.2%
Five governance polarised	2.3%	4.1%	2.3%	1.4%

Source: World Bank (2002: 15).

absence of any sustained acceleration in growth, and possibly even a trend decline. In sum, the data strongly suggest that, although important country-to-country variations are evident, adjustment contributes to an acceleration of aggregate economic growth and to productivity-improving changes in economic structure.

Governance Trends and Challenges

Table 2 summarises the responses to a question included in a 1996 survey of over 3600 firms in each of 69 countries (including 22 in Africa, 18 of which are included in the sample used in this chapter), conducted for the 1997 World Development Report, *The State in a Changing World* (World Bank, 1997). The countries were asked the following, to be answered both as of the time of the survey and as of 10 years earlier: 'Please rate your overall perception of the relation between government and/or bureaucracy and private firms on the following 6-point scale'.

Each firm scored its perceptions of the relationship on a 1–6 scale. A score of 1 signalled that government was perceived as a helping hand, and 6 signalled that it was an opponent. The difference between the proportion of respondents that scored the relationship 1 or 2 and the proportion that scored the relationship 5 or 6 provides one simple way to summarise the extent to which government is perceived as a net helping hand or opponent. In Ghana, for example, 48 per cent more firms reported that as of 1986 they perceived government to be an opponent than perceived government to be a helping hand. By contrast, for 1996, 39 per cent more firms perceived government as a helping hand than as an opponent. Table 2 summarises the results for 18 countries, organised into the three subgroups used in this article.

The results point to a remarkable turnaround between 1986 and 1996 among the sustained adjusters concerning the impact of public sector governance on the economy – an average gain in the net helping hand ratio of 54 per cent. In 1986 the ratio was negative in all seven countries; by 1996 it had become positive in five of the seven (and, although still net negative, had improved by 20 points or more in the remaining two). As for the other countries, the ratio had

Table 2. Trends in relations between private firms and government in 18 African countries, 1986–1996

Country	Net helping hand (+ve) or opponent (−ve)		
	1986	1996	Net change
Benin	−43	−23	+20
Ghana	−48	+39	+87
Malawi	−29	+17	+46
Mali	−29	+11	+40
Mozambique	−55	−19	+36
Uganda	−38	+37	+75
Zambia	−56	+19	+75
Average for sustained adjusters	*−43*	*+11*	*+54*
Cameroon	+7	−24	−31
Chad	0	−31	−31
Guinea	−10	−10	0
Madagascar	−37	−42	−5
Senegal	−8	−20	−12
Tanzania	−51	−36	+15
Average for later adjusters	*−16*	*−27*	*−11*
Cote d'Ivoire	−2	−16	−14
Kenya	−13	−2	−11
Nigeria	+61	+6	−55
Togo	+10	−21	−31
Zimbabwe	−24	−36	−12
Average for governance polarised	*+6*	*−14*	*−8*

Source: Survey conducted for World Bank, World Development Report 1997, *The State in a Changing World.*

worsened in four of the five governance polarised countries, as well as in four of the six later adjusters for which data were available; only Tanzania enjoyed significant gains, although still below those of the sustained adjusters. Note, though, that these governance gains appear to be founded on changes in expectations, rather than on actual improvements in the performance of public institutions. Thus the question arises, is this seemingly positive trend sustainable?

The comparative evidence reported in Table 3 on performance of the 21 African countries in controlling corruption highlights the concern. Data on corruption form a useful proxy for the quality of public institutions because they signal the extent to which these institutions can, first, constrain public actors from pursuing private ends and, second, direct private action aimed at influencing public officialdom to formal, rather than informal, channels. Although corruption is difficult to measure – and all measures are recognised as having wide margins of error – worldwide data provided by the World

Table 3. Control of corruption: comparative global rank of 21 African countries

	1996 percentile ranking	2002 percentile ranking
Sustained adjusters (average rank)	*31*	*31*
Benin	–	34
Burkina Faso	44	58
Ghana	36	43
Malawi	12	20
Mali	44	46
Mozambique	33	15
Uganda	32	16
Zambia	16	17
Later adjusters (average rank)	*39*	*33*
Cameroon	7	9
Chad	–	13
Guinea	66	36
Madagascar	66	62
Mauritania	–	63
Niger	44	8
Senegal	39	53
Tanzania	9	16
Governance polarised (average rank)	*31*	*15*
Cote d'Ivoire	72	23
Kenya	9	11
Nigeria	5	3
Togo	13	33
Zimbabwe	55	6

Bank Institute are widely regarded as among the most comprehensive and reliable (and careful, in so far as standard errors and point estimates are reported) available.[3] The data set is for over 150 countries for two-year periods from 1996 to 2002.

Table 3 reports the percentile rank in controlling corruption for each of the 21 African countries, relative to the worldwide population, for 1996 and for 2002. (A country in the 5th percentile is better at controlling corruption than only 4 per cent of the sample; by contrast a country in the 95th percentile is better than 94 per cent of the sample.) The results give little comfort concerning the quality of Africa's public institutions as of 1996, concerning their subsequent direction of change, or concerning any positive impact of economic reform on corruption:

• As of 2002 only six of the 21 countries ranked above the worst performing 40 per cent of countries worldwide in their control of corruption.

- The period from 1996 to 2002 shows no evidence of systematic improvement: only three countries improved their percentile ranking by 10 or more points, and the ranking worsened by at least that amount for six countries.
- As of 1996 sustained adjusters were no better at controlling corruption than other groups; and over the subsequent six-year period, although one country in the sustained adjuster group (Burkina Faso) improved by more than 10 points, the performance of two others (Mozambique and Uganda) worsened by at least that amount.

Overall, then, Africa's governance landscape as of the first decade of the twenty-first century offers a mixed picture. In the decades immediately following independence, a majority of countries succumbed to a downward governance spiral, characterised by perverse incentives on the part of political and economic actors and the corresponding decay of political and bureaucratic institutions. Beginning in the mid-1980s a combination of external pressure and internal discontent set in motion in many countries processes of economic and political liberalisation, which broke the iron grip of these perverse political incentives and their consequences for governance.

Even so, the transformation does not appear to have been dramatic enough to turn a vicious spiral into a virtuous one. The risks thus remain high that, in the absence of a continuing momentum of positive change, a downward spiral can readily reassert itself. Enhancing the capacity of political and bureaucratic institutions emerges as crucial for Africa's development prospects.

Strengthening Capacity and Accountability: Lessons from Specific Interventions

Efforts to help build state capacity in Africa are not new. For example, between 1987 and 1997 the World Bank implemented at least 70 civil service reform projects across the African continent (World Bank, 1999). The results of these interventions were mixed at best: of those completed by 1997, only 29 per cent were rated satisfactory in a review by the World Bank's arms-length Operations Evaluations Department.

Viewed through the lens of hindsight, a principal reason for the limited success of the first round of efforts to build state capacity was the implicit presumption that the weakness of public administration was managerial and could be remedied in a straightforward manner through a combination of organisational overhaul and financial support to procure the requisite specialist technical advice, training, and hardware. By contrast, consistent with the conceptual framework in this issue developed by Goetz, a central lesson of experience is that public administrations are embedded in a complex, interdependent system. This system incorporates not only the bureaucratic apparatus as a whole, but also social, economic, and political interests more broadly, and the political institutions which link the state and society. As Goetz highlights, the incentives of political leaders as to whether and how to proceed with governance reform are shaped by the institutional system as a whole – not just one part. State-building thus requires attention to the challenges of building both public administrative capability and the complementary institutions that hold the bureaucracy accountable for performance.

Building Bureaucratic Capability

This section reviews some findings of the impact across African countries of efforts at administrative reform, at pay policy reform, and reform of public expenditure management systems. As will become evident, the reviews yield a consistent set of lessons as to what works, what does not – and why.

Administrative reform

Engberg-Pedersen and Levy (2004) seek general patterns from the results of 15 World Bank-supported state capacity-building projects (implemented across 11 African countries). They find that comprehensive efforts at administrative reform achieved some success in only three of seven sample countries where they were attempted – Tanzania, plus two additional countries with a politically propitious environment (Cape Verde and Uganda), and have achieved little in the remaining four countries, where political constraints short-circuited ambitious programmes (Ghana, Zambia, Guinea and Kenya).

Stevens and Teggemann (2004) review comparatively public administration reform implementation experiences in Ghana, Tanzania, and Zambia. They confirm that, among the three countries, only in Tanzania was the political environment sufficiently favourable to warrant the pursuit of a comprehensive programme of administrative reform. And only in that country do the results seem to be fulfilling the programme's initial promise. Ghana's reforms barely went beyond the analytic phase before being put on hold following a change in government. Zambia made improvements in some limited areas and is intensifying its efforts toward a focused agenda for improving expenditure accountability. Thus, Stevens and Teggemann conclude that in countries (including, in hindsight, Ghana and Zambia) in which 'the political environment is less favourable, reform components need to be carefully selected and tailored to start with basic and politically less contentious reforms while creating opportunities for more comprehensive reform and generating momentum'.

Engberg-Pedersen and Levy (2004) report also on the relative effectiveness of different types of more narrowly focused reforms. Among these reforms, their sample reveals a striking difference in the performance of capacity-building initiatives focused on improving expenditure accountability (eight of their sample of nine components were rated successful) and those focused on human resource management (only two of eight components were rated successful). To account for this difference, Engberg-Pedersen and Levy suggest that large groups with vested interests and legitimate claims in the bureaucracy may perceive expenditure accountability activities as more technical and less threatening than the more politically sensitive administrative reforms, which may have more immediate redistributional consequences. They speculate that another reason might be the more readily observable results for expenditure accountability initiatives, and they provide extensive suggestions about how a results focus might more effectively and more broadly be incorporated into administrative reform and state capacity-building.

Pay policy reform

Public sector pay policy is key both for fiscal management and for public sector performance – and has been a preoccupation of African governments and their development partners (including the World Bank) for at least two decades. Kiragu *et al.* (2004) distinguish between technically rational, politically rational, and politically reactive approaches to pay policy and use these distinctions to review empirically the evolution of public sector pay in eight countries. Only Botswana has consistently sustained pay policies and outcomes that approximate accepted notions of good practice in this area. And only Tanzania and Uganda have managed to reroute politically reactive policies in more technically and politically rational directions. The remaining five countries (Benin, Burkina Faso, Ghana, Senegal, and Zambia) have been stuck in politically rational or reactive modes, although with some cross-country variation, including a few short-lived episodes of attempted reform.

Kiragu *et al.* (2004) link these differences in performance to differences across countries in the political constraints and opportunities for pay reform, specifically to cross-country variations in the characteristics of institutional actors, of political system and stability variables, and of civil society. They conclude that the capacity to adopt technically rational pay policies is greatest in settings that are characterised by high levels of political and administrative institutionalisation, but that have relatively low levels of political competition (that is, Botswana, Tanzania, and Uganda). By contrast, settings that have high levels of political competition but low institutionalisation (Benin, Ghana, and Zambia) seem especially prone to politically reactive approaches to pay reform. Taking a long-run institution-building perspective, they underscore the value of adopting pay policies that nurture and build institutions and governing coalitions, rather than those that risk being polarising.

Public expenditure management

The quality of national budget formulation, execution, and reporting has risen to the top of Africa's development agenda for two reasons. The first reason is the move to democracy, and the associated expectations that citizens have the right to hold governments accountable for how public resources are used. The second reason is the increased recognition by donors of the centrality of 'country ownership' to development effectiveness and a consequent desire to transfer donor resources to African countries in ways that support, rather than circumvent, national processes of prioritisation and oversight. As the chapters make clear, the realities on the ground fall far short of idealised, best practice approaches to budgeting.

Garnett and Plowden (2004) take as their point of departure the poverty reduction strategy paper (PRSP) process, which in many African countries has become an important basis for resource transfers by the World Bank, the International Monetary Fund and, increasingly, other donors as well. As Garnett and Plowden note, PRSPs generally have been participatory – but implementation depends on how well they are linked to ongoing policy-making processes of government. They highlight the budget as a key locus where general political promises are translated into concrete actions – and examine how the processes of budget formulation work in practice in Mozambique, South Africa, Uganda, and Zambia.

In all four countries, the finance ministry emerges as the leading player, but large variations are evident across countries both in its effectiveness and in the extent to which its decisions are embedded in a process that builds effective consensus among the leadership regarding the legitimacy of the result. Neither Zambia nor Mozambique has been able to implement effective processes for prioritisation. In Zambia an ad hoc supplementary budget appropriations process undercuts the initial budget almost to the point of irrelevancy. In Mozambique large-scale funding from donors, which (at least until very recently) has been separated from the national budget, has given de facto fiscal independence to favoured line ministries. Uganda, by contrast, has been highly effective in prioritising public spending, but its process has been controlled almost entirely by a dominant and capable Ministry of Finance, Planning, and Economic Development, which has enjoyed the firm backing of the powerful national president. Only in South Africa do Garnett and Plowden document a clear commitment to a more consensual prioritisation process, although this commitment, too, is a continuing evolution from the dominant finance-ministry model, which prevailed in the immediate post-apartheid period. In sum their case studies suggest that the road linking a participatory PRSP process to a genuinely inclusive and consensual process of budget formulation is, at best, a long and circuitous one.

Dorotinsky and Floyd (2004) report and reflect on the results of efforts to benchmark the quality of expenditure accountability systems in 20 African countries – not only budget formulation, but also budget execution and budget reporting. In 2001 staff of the World Bank, the International Monetary Fund, and 20 participating countries worked together to benchmark 15 distinct technical features of budgeting. The state of public expenditure management systems in many countries emerges as poor.

Budget formulation emerges as least problematic, relatively speaking. Two-thirds of the 20 countries meet at least half of the seven benchmarks in this area. By contrast, only 50 per cent of the countries meet at least two of the four budget execution benchmarks. To improve budget execution, almost three-quarters of the benchmarked countries have begun to invest in computerised financial management information systems. Dorotinsky and Floyd (2004) review the interaction between computerised financial management information system investments and the quality of budget execution, and they conclude that technology can add value only in the context of an underlying commitment to disciplined decision-making and internal management systems that are geared to monitoring compliance.

Budget reporting is highlighted as a core element of transparency, empowerment, and accountability but, because only 40 per cent of countries meet at least two of the four benchmarks in this area, it emerges as the weakest of the three areas. As Dorotinsky and Floyd (2004) highlight, many countries have put in place rules of the game that formally allow supreme audit institutions to scrutinise expenditures independently and report the results publicly. In practice, however, impact has been limited in the face of:

- public accounts that often are inaccurate, cover only part of public expenditures, and are made available only after long delays;
- supreme audit institutions that lack the skill base to do their job effectively;
- very uneven parliamentary oversight.

Yet for all the shortcomings of the previous status quo, Dorotinsky and Floyd (2004) find reasons to be hopeful that the 2001 benchmarking exercise might have been an important wake-up call. For one thing, a follow-up implementation update conducted in 2004 documented intensified country-level activity to fix the shortcomings, and significant progress was being made among the lowest rated countries. For another, the preoccupation with national budget systems reflects a growing willingness in principle on the part of donors to

provide aid in the more fungible form of budget support, and both the intensified efforts to strengthen national budget systems and the evident link between
stronger national budget systems and development effectiveness seem to be
helping accelerate this process. Finally, the intensified focus on expenditure
accountability comes at a time when development practitioners are acknowled-
ging the limitations of comprehensive public sector capacity-building efforts.
The risk is thus diminishing that efforts to improve expenditure accountability
will become lost in the crowd of an overloaded reform agenda.

A Consistent Tension – Best Practice versus Incrementalism

A similar logic underlies the analysis and experience of each of the administrative, pay policy and public expenditure management reform areas. For each,
there exists a well-understood set of mechanisms with the potential to align the
bureaucracy to support developmental goals. Taking these normative best
practices as the starting point and examining the degree to which they have
been realised in practice, a common pattern emerges: in all but a few cases
the results so far have fallen far short of the normative model.

The reasons for this implementation shortfall appear to be wholly consistent with the analytical framework used in this issue for the other case studies:
the need to balance the technocratic logic that shapes many proposals for
reform against the incentives that country-specific political and institutional
variables generate for reformers. These incentives include political imperatives of building and sustaining alliances with powerful patrons, of avoiding
conflict with powerful social groups, and of maintaining electoral support.
Depending on the severity of the political constraints, even well-intentioned
leaders are thus limited in how ambitious a reform agenda they can adopt. A
key lesson from the experiences with building administrative capability laid
out above is that it can be counterproductive for technocrats to ignore these
constraints and bulldoze along with an agenda of comprehensive best practice
solutions. In most countries the emphasis could more usefully be placed, first,
on approaches to administrative reform that are more partial and more tailored
to country-specific windows of opportunity and, second, on determined
follow-through to achieve results in the few areas selected for focused effort.

Strengthening Accountability

Because it has become clearer that the challenges of building state capacity are
at least as political as they are technical, the focus has intensified on the demand
side of capacity. The intent is to alter the incentives of political leaders by
reshaping state institutional arrangements in ways that require them increasingly
to respond to a broad array of civic pressures for performance and not simply to

the elites who benefited from the status quo. Three diverse arenas – parliaments, anti-corruption initiatives, and local governance – offer some rich lessons as to the prospects and challenges of strengthening accountability.

National parliaments

National parliaments have, in principle, a fundamental, dominant role in assuring horizontal accountability. The empirical investigation by Barkan *et al.* (2004) identified large disparities in the effectiveness of parliaments across four countries, all of which are formally democratic, and also within countries over time. The Kenyan Parliament of the past five years emerged as unequivocally the most independently assertive. The Ghanaian and Beninese legislatures are described as semi-independent and certainly more independent as of 2002 than 10–15 years earlier. The Senegalese legislature, however, continued to be almost entirely subservient to the executive. These variations in independence translate into variations in how parliamentarians allocate their time between policy-related and constituency-support activities. The Kenyans are the most (and the Senegalese are the least) preoccupied with policy-related activities. But, even in Kenya, real engagement with the budgeting process (as distinct from other aspects of policy-making) is limited, and even this engagement tends to focus narrowly on the implementation of spending commitments within the districts of individual members. A combination of constitutional rules and executive control over the timing of the process precludes significant parliamentary influence on budget formulation. Furthermore multi-year delays in the presentation of audits have led some parliamentarians to refer disparagingly to audit committees as the 'post-mortem committees'.

   To account for the observed variations in the effectiveness of parliaments, Barkan *et al.* focus on the impact of four distinct factors. First is the consistent pull, evident in all countries, toward patronage-driven, deliver-the-goods-to-constituents behaviour by legislators – a result of the rural, local-geography-focused organisation of political interests. Second are differences in formal rules, which Barkan *et al.* acknowledge explain part – although they insist only a modest part – of the cross-country variations. The third factor, which they highlight as a powerful proximate source of variation across countries, comprises cross-country differences in the pay and institutional resources available to parliamentarians. They note, though, that the level of resources available to legislators is unlikely to rise unless forcefully demanded by the legislators themselves. They argue that the composition of legislatures has shifted in favour of 'reformers' and opportunistic 'patronage-seekers' at the expense of 'incumbent authoritarians', and they link this shift to a combination of a generational change (younger legislators are better educated and more globally connected), the rise of civic activism among urban elites, and the rise of multi-party democracy across Africa. Because they locate the changes in legislative performance in the assertiveness of legislators themselves, and because they link this assertiveness to shifts in legislator composition as a result of domestic social changes, Barkan *et al.* conclude on the cautionary note that 'the modernisation of the African legislature ... cannot be "orchestrated" from outside' (2004).

Anti-corruption Campaigns

Kpundeh (2004) reviews recent initiatives across Africa to combat corruption; anticorruption emerged in the mid-1990s as an especially potent means of mobilising civic energy for good government. Kpundeh distinguishes between structural interventions aimed at strengthening the capacity, transparency, and accountability of state institutions and softer process interventions. The latter include efforts to mobilise civic pressure for change (for example, by documenting transparently the extent of the corruption problem); working to reshape the attitudes of public officials; and engaging in high-profile, but often ad hoc and politically opportunistic, actions to crack down on corrupt political and bureaucratic leaders. Much of the energy in the late 1990s focused exclusively on these process interventions, and Kpundeh highlights the risk that they raise expectations rapidly, but fail to deliver – and thereby end up fuelling cynicism rather than reform.

Dedicated anticorruption agencies frequently are established as a quick-fix response to the problem. Kpundeh (2004) examines their impact through the lens of the structure–process dichotomy; he notes very different trajectories across countries. Botswana's Directorate for Corruption and Economic Crimes operates against the backdrop of strong complementary state institutions and is a useful part of the overall arsenal of tools to ensure that public resources are well used. By contrast, Malawi's Anti-Corruption Bureau and Sierra Leone's Anti-Corruption Commission are criticised as 'phony populist' mechanisms – typical examples of process interventions meant to give the appearance of action while changing little. Tanzania's Prevention of Corruption Bureau, Uganda's Inspectorate of Government, and Zambia's Anti-Corruption Commission (that is, since that country's change of presidential leadership in 2002; earlier it had been a typical example of phony populism) occupy an intriguing intermediate space. They are effective mechanisms for combating corruption in the short term, en route to more far-reaching comprehensive reforms of the public sector.

According to Kpundeh (2004) a combination of, first, strong top-level leadership (including the readiness and authority to override opposition from otherwise influential elites) and, second, a sustained partnership with civilian actors committed to opposing corruption distinguishes the more effective short-term transitional mechanisms from their phony populist counterparts. More broadly he concludes that the most effective way forward in the fight against corruption appears to be through a dynamic interaction between process and structural interventions, with the intent of initiating a virtuous cycle of improving pressure for change, and responsiveness to that pressure.

Decentralisation and Local Governance

The political and economic virtues of democratic decentralisation are perceived by its advocates to be far-reaching. The political virtues include, first, restraining arbitrary action by national leadership by expanding the number of check-and-balance points built into the constitutional framework and, second, deepening democracy and citizen empowerment by providing focal points at all levels of society for civic contestation. The economic virtues include, first, improving allocative efficiency by shifting decisions about how to prioritise down to the lowest feasible level and, second, improving the productivity of public resources by creating more direct mechanisms for citizen-users to pressure public officials for improved performance. The extent to which achievement of this ambitious agenda is consistent with the political realities on the ground is a key empirical question.

Ndegwa and Levy (2004) use case studies of Malawi, Senegal, and Uganda to explore in depth the political dynamics of decentralisation. As they show, for a rapid and sustained decentralisation to proceed effectively, a formidable set of enabling political conditions needs to be in place. Uganda came closest to meeting these, but even there the process proceeded in a way that left local governments potentially subordinate to central authorities (even in areas where responsibility was formally assigned to the local level). In Malawi and Senegal, the political conditions were more constraining and had corresponding limitations in the extent to which, at least so far, local governments have been empowered. Malawi's high-profile Malawi Social Action Fund (MASAF) illustrates the ambiguities nicely.[4] Since its inception in 1995, MASAF has made available well over US$100 million for local infrastructure investments. By all accounts, the resources have been used effectively, cost efficiently, and in ways that have been empowering to local communities. What remains unclear, though, is whether MASAF will turn out to be an important stepping stone to genuinely accountable local government or if it will ossify as a populist centrally controlled vehicle for winning support for the incumbent political leadership.[5]

The Malawi and Senegal case studies lead Ndegwa and Levy (2004) to a variety of propositions about how to proceed with reforms to foster downward accountability in politically constrained settings. First, they suggest that at least as much attention should be given to building the requisite political coalitions for change as to refining the technical details of optimal decentralisation. The case studies suggest that Senegal, and perhaps Malawi, may have fallen into the trap of analysis as a substitute for action. Second, in politically constrained settings, they advocate greater openness to heterodox, institutionally messy initiatives that strengthen downward accountability and that can spur forward the process of political change.

Ndegwa and Levy (2004) underscore the importance of getting the balance right between pragmatism and vision – not just vis-à-vis decentralisation, but more broadly. On the one hand, a preoccupation with technical best practice approaches can lead to paralysis, and to the neglect of politically feasible options. But the opposite also holds true: an exclusive preoccupation with quick fixes at the frontline, without attention to overall system coherence as well, is likely eventually to prove unsustainable – both because of the ad hoc nature of the technical arrangements for resource flows and, more fundamentally, because without more broadly institutionalised checks and balances, changes in political winds too readily overwhelm ad hoc innovations.

A Consistent Pattern – Accountability-building as a Cumulative Process

As with administrative reform, the tension between best practice and political realities emerges as a central theme in the experience with efforts to strengthen accountability. But something more is evident.

The discussion of local governance suggests strongly that looking only for the opportunity for incremental improvement is insufficient. For countries committed to improving local governance, by virtue of both its institutional coherence and the way in which it locks in a transformation of how power and resources flow through the polity, a well-functioning formal intergovernmental system should remain the guiding North Star to which more pragmatic and diverse strategies adopted in the short and medium term should converge over time. What seems to be called for, then, is a creative response to opportunities as they emerge, never losing sight of, but not being paralysed by, the long-run imperatives of overall institutional coherence.

The aim is a virtuous cycle which progressively transforms both performance and accountability. Though not (yet) evident in work on decentralisation, just such a cycle may be coming into view vis-à-vis strengthened accountability for budgetary spending:

- The earlier discussion of public expenditure management highlighted the weaknesses in many African countries of ex-post-audit systems, but noted that (given recent improvements in the legal framework) some straightforward ways of getting improvements exist and pointed also to rising interest among donors to provide the requisite support (as part of the broader interest in expenditure accountability).

- In the discussion of parliaments, implicit in the finding that parliamentarians disparage the 'post-mortem' audit committee is the prospect that, if audits were more timely and of higher quality, with greater likelihood of follow-up by the executive, the function of budget oversight would be taken more seriously.
- The discussion of anticorruption pointed to an increasing focus on leveraging constructive changes in transparency and accountability institutions, rather than on quick-gratification statements of intent accompanied by politically ambiguous efforts to fry a big fish, so to speak.

It follows that actions to strengthen supreme audit institutions, to intensify civic interest and engagement in how public resources actually are used, and to support parliamentary efforts to strengthen their expenditure oversight functions are potentially mutually reinforcing. More reliable, timely, and transparent information and the resulting intensified scrutiny on public spending can provide momentum for investment in systems to improve expenditure accountability. The resulting improvements in transparency can, in turn, make civic activism more effective. More effective activists can press parliamentarians to perform better – and better-functioning parliaments provide valuable points of leverage for activists. Parliaments are also mutually reinforcing in relation to systems of expenditure accountability. Better systems to account for how public monies are used enable parliamentarians to do their job better, and empowered parliamentarians are better positioned to push for improved information from the bureaucracy. If a virtuous spiral can be initiated across these different dimensions of expenditure accountability, the cumulative consequence even of some relatively limited initial actions could be far-reaching improvements in the accountability of the public sector and thereby progressively in public performance.

Governance Reform – an Integrated Approach

The similar lessons extracted in the previous section from a diversity of administrative and accountability reform experiences underscore the value of a broad conceptual framework along the lines laid out by Goetz in this issue. Such a framework helps shift the attention of governance reformers from a narrow focus on organisational and public management approaches to a broader, integrated perspective that incorporates both the institutional rules of the game within which public organisations operate and the political dynamics.

Four propositions highlight how this integrated perspective reshapes the discourse of governance reform. Moving progressively more upstream from the bureaucratic frontline, these propositions are the following:

- First, bureaucracies are agents of political principals; political principals set objectives, which bureaucracies are charged with implementing.

It follows that the behaviour of public bureaucracies cannot be understood without attention to their politically derived objectives, and that the capacities of public bureaucracies cannot effectively be built in isolation from broader systemic changes, including strengthening the mechanisms for clarifying political purposes and communicating them to bureaucracies.

- Second, improvements in systems of accountability strengthen pressure for performance on public actors.

It follows that an important focus of efforts to improve public performance should be on building the capacities of accountability systems. These capacities include (a) hierarchical control structures within bureaucracies, (b) downwardly accountable governance structures through which elected political leaders monitor bureaucratic behaviour and through which citizens provide feedback to politicians, and (c) downward accountability mechanisms that link citizen-users more directly to providers of services.

- Third, the political institutions and the structure of political interests that underpin systems of accountability are country-specific, so efforts to build state capacity need a good fit with country-specific realities.

It follows that the approach to building state capacity cannot be an undifferentiated, best practice, cookie-cutter approach. Key, rather, is understanding country-specific constitutional structures and patterns of political, social, and economic interests and to aim for a good fit between efforts to strengthen administrative and accountability systems and these country-specific realities.

- Fourth, change processes can be cumulative.

This proposition follows directly from the fact of interdependence. Change in any one part of the system potentially induces change in other parts as well. It directs attention toward the identification of entry points for reform and capacity-building, which, although modest in themselves, have the potential to catalyse further changes down the road and thereby to expand progressively the opportunities for building state capacity.

Table 4. Governance reform – an integrated approach

	I		II
Analytical orientation	Technical	⇔	Political
	Supply	⇔	Demand
Focus Areas	Bureaucracy	⇔	Oversight Mechanisms
	Central	⇔	Local
Design principles	Best Practice	⇔	Next Steps, Good Fit
	Comprehensive	⇔	Focused, Results-oriented
	Structure	⇔	Process

Table 4 contrasts a traditional, technocratic, and managerial approach to building state capacity, depicted in column I, with the modifications, depicted in column II, that come from incorporating into the framework a broader institutional and political perspective. The role of the two-way arrows warrants emphasising: the emerging challenge is to harness the necessary, specialist public management expertise highlighted in column I to processes of change management, which are embedded in a clear-sighted view of the underlying drivers of political and institutional change highlighted in column II. Put differently, the integrated perspective represents an extension and refinement of earlier efforts – *not* their abandonment.

Three sets of contrasts between the technocratic and integrated perspectives are highlighted in Table 4. The first contrast is in analytical orientation. The technocratic approach bestows privileges to specialist knowledge of the details of how public administrative systems function and has a corresponding analytical focus on how to enhance the supply and use of human resources. The new approach requires also a skill in analysing country-specific political institutions and dynamics and, based on that analysis, identifying potential entry points for enhancing demand for improved public performance.

The second contrast is in the areas of focus. The integrated approach expands the focus areas beyond central bureaucracies to include the oversight mechanisms for holding bureaucracies accountable and also, because of the enhanced opportunities afforded at community level for direct citizen participation and oversight, the institutional arrangements for public action at sub-national and local levels.

The third contrast is in the design principles underlying governance reform. A typical traditional programme attempted to emulate best practice structures in industrialised countries (commonly, in the 1990s, the New Zealand model). Often, it also attempted comprehensive reform, on the presumption that a chain is only as strong as its weakest link. The integrated approach works to modify best practice to achieve a good fit with country-specific realities.

Sequencing emerges in the integrated approach as central. Given country-specific realities, what is likely to be the most effective way forward? How should that strategy prioritise and sequence across the various arenas for possible engagement? The answers from the comparative review of African reform experiences are strikingly similar to those that emerged from the comparative case studies of Brazil, India and Uganda described elsewhere in this issue.

In some countries, the starting points for further enhancement of state capacity are strong. Political leadership has a clear developmentally oriented vision and a mandate for acting on that vision. A workable baseline of bureaucratic capabilities exists. Such settings provide the opportunity for embarking on a comprehensive programme of state capacity-building, as exemplified by Tanzania's programme of administrative reform and capacity-building.

A second group of countries comprises those that have been part of Africa's democratic opening and that enjoy political stability, but that continue to operate largely along neo-patrimonial lines. A consistent message is that, in such countries, comprehensive programmes of state capacity-building are certain to fail. What is called for instead is some modest initial steps to identify, and build on, entry points for governance reform that, although modest in themselves, have the potential to set in motion far-reaching cumulative changes.

The bulk of countries have an uneven landscape of reformers and neo-patrimonials and lie more to the middle of the spectrum between bureaucratic capability and bureaucratic dysfunction. For this group, the opportunities for reform and capacity-building will be spread idiosyncratically across the institutional landscape, driven by where the champions happen to be active. Promising examples summarised earlier include: the strong positive impact on policy prioritisation of Uganda's investment in the capacity of its Ministry of Finance, Planning, and Economic Development; Malawi's social fund; Kenya's Parliament; and the array of World Bank-supported expenditure accountability operations. As all of these examples attest, the key to moving forward is a readiness to live with messiness and with imperfection in relation to ideal technical designs, but at the same time not to lose sight of the overall, more coherent, long-run constellation of state capacities and institutional interrelationships toward which the individual efforts are headed.

In sum, the central message of this paper is that governance reformers must find a middle ground between the bipolar moods that have for decades plagued developmental theory and practice: exuberant optimism that some magic formula for development has been found, followed inevitably by deep disappointment over its limitations. By contrast, the way forward outlined here might best be described as hopeful realism. Realism, in the recognition that only in a few African countries (and, even there, perhaps only for a limited period of time) is the way forward likely to yield major gains in the short term. The world over, the work of building states that are both effective and accountable to their citizens is a centuries-long process; Africa's independence from colonial rule came less than half a century ago. And hope in the conviction that, irrespective of a country's initial circumstance, some way forward for building state capacity is there to be tapped. Indeed, the process of cumulative causation points to the possibility that small beginnings can set in motion progressively more profound consequences.

Notes

1. Beginning with the full set of 48 sub-Saharan African countries, three sets of outlier countries were excluded: very small countries, countries affected by profound internal conflict, and the current middle-income, consistently high-performing countries. Furthermore, to facilitate comparison with earlier analysis, the selection of countries was limited to those that were included in the 1994 World Bank study, *Adjustment in Africa.*
2. The World Bank (2002) reports directly the growth rates for 1975–84, 1985–89, and 1990–2000, and annual data for 1991–2000. This chapter used the 1991, 1996, and 2000 data to calculate growth rates for the sub-periods 1991–96 and 1996–2000. The gap in information between 1989 and 1991 is an artefact of the way the data were made available and has no implication for the patterns detailed in Table 1 and the text (based on inspection of the 1990–2000 growth rates, not reported here).
3. Access to these data is available at http://www.Worldbank.org/wbi. For details of the data set and methodology, see Kaufmann *et al.* (1999).
4. Social funds along MASAF lines have been used in more than a dozen African countries, including on a large scale, Eritrea, Ethiopia, Ghana, Guinea, Madagascar, Nigeria, Senegal, Tanzania, and Zambia.
5. Although none of the other African countries that have social funds yet provides guidance in this regard, the contrasting experience of two Latin American countries, Bolivia and Peru, is revealing. Peru's social fund became progressively more closely tied to the office of President Fujimori, part of a populist machine, but with no long-term gains for institution-building. By contrast, Bolivia successfully used the empowerment structures nurtured through its social fund to build unusually robust mechanisms of downward accountability when it promulgated its Popular Participation Law, which shifted control of the resources to newly empowered local governments.

References

Barkan, J., Adamolekun, L. & Zhou, Y. (2004) Emerging legislatures: institutions of horizontal accountability, in: B. Levy & S. Kpundeh (Eds) *Building State Capacity in Africa* (Washington, DC: World Bank).

Bratton, M. & van de Walle, D. (1997) *Democratic Experiments in Africa* (Cambridge: Cambridge University Press).

Dia, M. (1996) *Africa's management in the 1990s and beyond: reconciling indigenous and transplanted institutions*, Directions in Development Series (Washington, DC: World Bank).

Dorotinsky, B. & Floyd, R. (2004) 'Public expenditure accountability in Africa: progress, lessons, and challenges', in: B. Levy & S. Kpundeh (Eds) *Building State Capacity in Africa* (Washington, DC: World Bank).

Engberg-Pedersen, P. & Levy, B. (2004) Building state capacity in Africa: learning from performance and results', in: B. Levy & S. Kpundeh (Eds) *Building State Capacity in Africa* (Washington, DC: World Bank).

Garnett, H. & Plowden, W. (2004) Cabinets, budgets, and poverty: political commitment to poverty reduction, in: B. Levy & S. Kpundeh (Eds) *Building State Capacity in Africa* (Washington, DC: World Bank).

Kaufmann, D., Kraay, A. & Zoido-Lobaton, P. (1999) *Governance Matters*, World Bank Policy Research Department Working Paper No. 2196 (Washington, DC: World Bank).

Kiragu, K., Mukandala, R. & Morin, D. (2004) Reforming pay policy: techniques, sequencing, and politics, in: B. Levy & S. Kpundeh (Eds) *Building State Capacity in Africa* (Washington, DC: World Bank).

Kpundeh, S. (2004) Process interventions versus structural reforms: institutionalising anticorruption reforms in Africa, in: B. Levy & S. Kpundeh (Eds) *Building State Capacity in Africa* (Washington, DC: World Bank).

Levy, B. & Kpundeh, S. (Eds) (2004) *Building State Capacity in Africa: New Approaches, Emerging Lessons* (Washington, DC: World Bank Institute Development Studies).

Lewis, P. (1996) Economic reform and political transition in Africa: the quest for a politics of development, *World Politics*, 49(1), pp. 92–129.

Migdal, J. S. (1988) *Strong Societies and Weak States: State–Society Relations and State Capabilities in the Third World* (Princeton, NJ: Princeton University Press).

Moore, B. Jr. (1966) *Social Origins of Dictatorship and Democracy* (Boston, MA: Beacon Press).

Ndegwa, S. N. & Levy, B. (2004) The politics of decentralisation in Africa: a comparative analysis, in: B. Levy & S. Kpundeh (Eds) *Building State Capacity in Africa* (Washington, DC: World Bank).

North, D. (1990) *Institutions, Institutional Change and Economic Performance* (New York: Cambridge University Press).

Stevens, M. & Teggemanr, S. (2004) Comparative experience with public service sector reform in Ghana, Tanzania, and Zambia, in: B. Levy & S. Kpundeh (Eds) *Building State Capacity in Africa* (Washington, DC: World Bank).

Wood, A. (2002) Could Africa be like America? Paper presented at 14th annual World Bank Conference on Development Economics, 1994, Adjustment in Africa (Washington, DC: World Bank).

World Bank (1994) *Adjustment in Africa: Reform, Results and the Road Ahead* (New York: Oxford University Press for the World Bank).

World Bank (1997) *World Development Report 1997: The State in a Changing World* (New York: Oxford University Press).

World Bank (1999) *Civil Service Reform: A Review of World Bank Assistance*, Operations Evaluation Department, Report No. 19211 (Washington, DC: World Bank).

World Bank (2002) *African Development Indicators* (Washington, DC: World Bank).

The Politics of Successful Governance Reforms: Lessons of Design and Implementation

MARK ROBINSON

Governance and Conflict, UK Department for International Development

Introduction

Most existing analysis of public sector governance reforms focuses on the obstacles to successful implementation, including political resistance, bureaucratic inertia, and capacity constraints. A decade of experience has demonstrated that technocratic approaches to governance reform are limited in their scope and effectiveness. The implementation of governance reforms can be thwarted by inadequate attention to political factors and the importance of bureaucratic incentives for reform. There is a need to improve understanding of successful approaches by drawing lessons from the design and implementation of governance reforms designed to promote structural changes in state institutions and from the pattern of incentives that shapes the behaviour of politicians and bureaucrats.

This article examines the political and institutional factors that contribute to successful outcomes through comparative analysis of nine cases of governance reforms in Brazil, India and Uganda. The nine case studies cover four areas of public sector governance reform: public financial management (fiscal management and tax administration), anti-corruption, civil service reform, and innovations in service delivery. The article builds on country-specific insights into the conditions for successful reform centred on the incentives for reform on the part of political leaders and government officials. The case studies are rooted in an analysis of political dynamics and institutional factors, structural features of politics and society, and design and implementation variables in each country.

The findings highlight three factors essential to successful reform: the nature of political agency; the degree of technical capacity; and the timing and sequencing of reforms. Political commitment at the highest level of government supports officials responsible for reform implementation and helps diffuse opposition from those who may lose out by reform. A high degree of bureaucratic technical capacity, combined with some initial insulation from political and societal pressures, is conducive to sustainable reform. In addition, incremental reforms tend to be more effective than swift, wholesale measures.

The conclusion considers the wider implications of the research by highlighting the political and institutional factors that shape successful reform outcomes in different contexts. It suggests that explicit attention to the political feasibility of reform, helping to identify and build incentives for reform, and working with reform-oriented politicians and bureaucrats, is a fruitful approach for donor agencies to pursue.[1] This approach highlights the value of modest financial outlays that have the potential for scaling-up over time, supported by flexible lending instruments that respond to domestically driven reform agendas and build on incremental progress.

Conceptual Framework

The definition of governance adopted in this article builds on the formulation proposed by Campos and Pradhan as the manner in which the state acquires and exercises the authority to manage public goods and services (Campos & Pradhan, 2005: 1). Institutions are defined as sets of rules that shape the roles, behaviours, and expectations of social, political, and economic actors. These may be formally codified or have informal attributes grounded in kinship, ethnicity, and personal ties. The governance reforms examined in this article are reforms to the institutions that influence the behaviour of state actors, providing them with incentives to act in ways that improve the provision of public goods and services. They encompass reforms that are intended to promote structural changes in state institutions, through improvements in public expenditure management, civil service reform, the delivery of services, and the promotion of accountability.[2]

The conceptual framework developed by Goetz (this issue) is founded on the premise that successful design and implementation are a function of the formal and informal institutions that shape the incentives for decision-makers to initiate governance reforms. The decision of political leaders to embark on a governance reform strategy entails a careful assessment of the potential risks and benefits. The principal risks are a potential loss of patronage resources (in the form of public sector employment and rents) and a possible erosion of political support in response to unpopular measures. These are balanced by potential benefits in the form of enhanced electoral dividends resulting from improved economic performance and provision of goods and services. In this framework, the extent to which politicians are prepared to modify their patronage methods and resources is an important influence on reform outcomes. By extension, the incentives that discourage bureaucrats from impeding reform initiatives are integral to successful implementation.

The incentive structures governing reform implementation are fashioned by three sets of political and institutional factors: the *political institutions* that shape the choices made by political and bureaucratic actors, with a focus on the legislative domain and informal institutions rooted in family, kinship, and personal ties; the *connections between state and society* through which the compliance of non-state actors to reform is garnered, with particular emphasis on the role played by political parties and civil society organisations; and the *political agency* required to package reforms, moderate their scope and pace, and identify levels and arenas at which to begin, so that resistance is undermined and support cultivated. This highlights the importance of political leadership and commitment and the political skills required to design and manage risky reforms.

Drawing largely on the experience of successful developmental states, the conceptual framework that provides a reference point for the articles in this issue focuses attention on the key institutional and policy design features that enable reformers to downplay political threats, broker the formation of pro-reform coalitions, cushion the shock of reforms, and make reforms more palatable by delivering tangible benefits. The structural features of politics and society influence the capacity of decision-makers to embark on reforms, either in undercutting the privileges of elites accustomed to seeking rents through the state, or in enabling reformers to generate support from groups likely to benefit from reform.

Three structural features of politics and society that have a potential bearing on reform implementation are identified: (1) *Institutional depth:* greater longevity, flexibility, adaptability, and legitimacy of formal and informal institutions through which agreements are reached between contending social groups, or through which losers are compensated, strengthens support for reform and lowers the cost of innovation; (2) *Composition of governing elites*: the extent to which traditional (especially rural landholding) elites can inhibit the emergence of pro-poor coalitions and the ascendancy of new social groups committed to reform; and (3) *Diversity and depth of civil society*: a diverse civil society with institutions capable of developing horizontal solidarities can provide incentives to reformers by responding positively to reforms and offering new sources of political support to offset the loss of established constituencies opposed to reform.

Finally, the conceptual framework identifies four design and implementation variables that have a bearing on reform outcomes:

1. *Sequencing, timing and pace of reform*: reforms can be designed to generate early 'winners' who can support follow-on reforms or dissipate resistance through a gradualist approach that builds public support. Rapid and ambitious reforms can attract public support but also provoke political and bureaucratic resistance.
2. *Technical capacity*: public sector capacity constraints can blunt the implementation and impact of reforms that are championed by political leaders and command public support. The creation of autonomous state institutions with high technical capacity can foster effective implementation but also weaken the capacity and commitment of existing government bureaucracies.
3. *Devolution to sub-national governments*: the devolution of responsibility for some reforms to lower levels of government can deflect some of the opposition to reform, and also encourage experimentation and competition between different levels of government to maximise political gains from reform.
4. *'Monitorability' of reform*: the commitment of governments to reform measures is contingent on their openness to public scrutiny and legislative oversight. Public accountability measures may assist in sustaining reform momentum by containing opposition from vested interests.

In sum, the conceptual framework rests on a simple proposition: the design and implementation of governance reforms depends on the way that decision-makers respond to incentives shaped by political and institutional variables that are specific to reform content and regime context. Strategies for managing reform implementation range from the active pursuit of reform to diminish patronage and leverage political benefits, to a more risk-averse approach that favours incremental change and continued, selective investment in patronage systems to minimise potential dissent and the derailing of reform initiatives.

Governance Reforms in Brazil, India, and Uganda

Brazil, India, and Uganda were selected to illustrate successful reform implementation in three different political and institutional settings: respectively a transitional federal democracy with a presidential system; an established parliamentary federal democracy at state and national levels; and a presidential system with no-party elections. A range of reforms was examined in each country to reflect variations in the type of reform and the political context. They are intended to be representative of the major thrust of governance reform efforts from the late 1990s and embody the more successful initiatives pursued by these governments. Two sets of reforms centre on public expenditure management, in the form of changes in tax policy and administration in Brazil and Uganda, and the Fiscal Responsibility Law in Brazil. Civil service reform and anti-corruption initiatives are the focus of two of the Ugandan case studies. Innovations in service delivery in the two south Indian states of Karnataka and Andhra Pradesh include improvements to water supply through reforms to Metro Water in Hyderabad and the Development of Women and Children in Rural Areas (DWCRA) programme in Andhra Pradesh, and municipal reforms through the Bangalore Agenda Task Force and the *Bhoomi* scheme for computerising land records in Karnataka. The type, purpose, modality, and impact of the reforms that constitute the focus of the nine case studies are set out in Table 1.

The case studies focus on examples of successful reform, characterised by improved outcomes (such as rates of tax collection and the quality of service delivery) or institutional innovations that have the potential to contribute to improved outcomes (for example anti-corruption agencies, tax authorities, and fiscal policy initiatives). In some cases reforms primarily intended to bring about improvements in one area (such as service delivery) also produced other benefits (such as improved accountability and transparency). In several cases the observed successes were qualified in certain respects: increased tax capacity but greater inefficiency and inequality (tax reform in Brazil); significant institutional innovation but modest improvement in outcomes (the *Bhoomi* scheme in Karnataka); and lack of sustainability and/or reversals (civil service reform in Uganda).

The reform initiatives varied considerably in their scope, in terms of the number of agencies or sectors they were intended to affect, and the degree of change they sought to induce, ranging from small-scale incremental reform to large-scale structural change. They also varied in the speed and

Table 1. Case studies of governance reforms in Brazil, India and Uganda

Reform type	Reform purpose	Implementing agency	Reform outcome
Brazil			
Fiscal Responsibility Law	To establish limits on expenditure and borrowing by state governments	Federal Ministry of Planning, Budget and Management	Reductions in fiscal imbalances and improved accountability
Tax reform	To improve the efficiency of tax collection and to increase tax revenues	Federal Ministry of Planning, Budget and Management	Increased revenues but greater inefficiency and inequity
India			
Municipal reforms (Bangalore, Karnataka)	To improve the functioning of municipal agencies through consultation with a forum representing the private sector and professionals	Bangalore Agenda Task Force (BATF)	Improved operations and greater public accountability, improvements in municipal taxation and budgetary control
Municipal water supply (Hyderabad, Andhra Pradesh)	To improve the efficiency of municipal water supplies through management reforms	Metro Water	Improved water supply, enhanced complaints redressal system
Bhoomi Scheme: computerisation of land records (Karnataka)	To improve the management of land records for farmers	Revenue Department, Government of Karnataka	Improved speed and efficiency of transactions, reduced cost and lower levels of corruption

Development of Women and Children in Rural Areas (DWCRA) (Karnataka)	To improve the supply of micro-credit and other services to rural women	Department of Rural Development, Government of Andhra Pradesh	Improved delivery of micro-credit and other services and increased accountability
Uganda			
Civil service reforms	To improve the efficiency and capacity of the civil service through downsizing, ministerial restructuring and pay reforms	Ministry of Public Service, Government of Uganda	Reduction in numbers of civil servants and ministries and improvements in salaries; reductions in establishment costs not achieved, living wage not achieved
Creation of an independent tax body – Uganda Revenue Authority (URA)	To increase tax revenues through improved management efficiency and reduced corruption	Ministry of Finance, Planning, and Economic Development, Government of Uganda	Initial increases in tax revenues and reduction of corruption but not sustained
Creation of anti-corruption agencies	To tackle the problem of corruption in the public service and government institutions	Ministry of Ethics and Integrity; Inspectorate of Government; Office of the Auditor General	Creation of independent agencies; limited progress in reducing corruption through identification and prosecution of corrupt officials

intensity of implementation, from incremental reforms that built up over time to comprehensive or wholesale reform initiatives that were introduced relatively quickly. These dimensions of reform have a bearing on trajectories of implementation in different political and institutional settings.

In Brazil the success of the Fiscal Responsibility Law lies in an institutional innovation which promotes improved fiscal management. In contrast, the Brazilian tax reforms led to significantly enhanced revenues but left underlying institutional conditions unchanged. The reforms in the two Indian states were primarily intended to improve service delivery but also had a positive impact in other areas in the form of tackling corruption and improving accountability. The proposals of the Bangalore Agenda Task Force (BATF) led to some improvements in municipal taxation and public accountability. The reform of Metro Water in Hyderabad improved water supply and the management of public finance. The *Bhoomi* scheme in Karnataka greatly enhanced transparency and the efficiency of the administration of land records. The Development of Women and Children in Rural Areas (DWCRA) scheme in Karnataka provided rural women with improved access to credit through the formation of self-help groups, and improved the accountability of local government officials. Civil service reforms in Uganda reduced the number of civil servants and ministries and raised salaries, although the efficiency gains that resulted are difficult to quantify. The creation of the Uganda Revenue Authority contributed to a significant increase in revenues but did not contain corruption. New institutions designed to tackle corruption in Uganda were successfully established but produced modest results.

The cases of successful governance reforms in Brazil, India, and Uganda can be situated in the broader context of reform efforts in each country. A key governance challenge in Brazil emanates from the considerable powers granted to states for taxation, expenditure, and administration under the 1988 Constitution. Devolution of fiscal responsibilities to state governments resulted in a steady increase in the public service payroll and mounting debt as they struggled to perform functions previously assigned to the federal government. Effective monitoring of state fiscal policies by federal authorities was undermined by weaknesses in the political party system that encouraged self-interested behaviour by state politicians. A related governance challenge lies in the system of tax administration and the difficulties faced by the federal government in mobilising revenues in the face of high levels of state fiscal autonomy and in tackling the highly regressive nature of the Brazilian tax system. This provides the context for the two case studies of the Fiscal Responsibility Law and reform of tax administration and underlines their centrality in governance reform efforts in Brazil (Schneider, this issue).

Several modest, incremental, governance reforms pursued by the governments of Andhra Pradesh and Karnataka constitute the focus of three case studies from southern India, respectively premised on greater citizen involvement in monitoring service delivery in Hyderabad, municipal governance reform in Bangalore, and women's self-help groups in rural Karnataka. The *Bhoomi* scheme, by comparison, provides an example of an e-governance initiative undertaken by the Government of Karnataka to provide farmers with a computerised system for processing land records.

By the mid-1980s Uganda exhibited features of a failed state, following years of violent conflict, in which the government was unable to guarantee the security of its citizens and provide them with a basic level of services. It has managed to achieve considerable turnaround in the intervening years, with sustained economic growth rates, improved service delivery, and significant reduction in poverty. Governance reforms played a key role in the policy initiatives pursued by the no-party Movement regime. The Uganda case focuses on three reform initiatives designed to address problems of corruption and capacity in the public service: the creation of an independent revenue authority; civil service reform; and anti-corruption measures (Robinson, this issue).

Case Study Findings: Explaining Successful Implementation

The remainder of this section summarises the case study findings, demonstrating how these validate or question the premises of the conceptual framework and drawing out the factors that influence successful implementation in a range of political and institutional contexts. Despite variations in design and scope the reforms examined in the country case studies exhibit some common features. The evidence shows that successful governance reforms rest on a combination of political commitment, sound technical design, and incremental implementation. Other factors also play a role in shaping reform outcomes in the context of specific reforms under different types of political regime, but do not apply across the country cases and reform areas. These are summarised in Table 2.

Political Institutions

Political institutions perform an important role in the implementation of successful governance reforms under different regime types. The durability and longevity of these institutions also has a bearing on reform implementation. An expectation that political institutions will endure can enhance confidence in public policy decisions and help to build the credibility and predictability of the reform process under democratic as well as non-democratic regimes, though it can also create inertia and resistance to change.

A democratic political context in Brazil and India gives rise to a pattern of politics in which incentive structures are strongly shaped by a careful assessment of the costs and benefits of reform by political leaders. President Cardoso

Table 2. The conceptual framework and the case study reforms

	Uganda	Brazil	India
Political and institutional factors			
Political institutions	Presidential, no-party Movement system with elections	Presidential system with elected federal and state governments	Parliamentary system with elected central and state governments
Connections between state and society	Limited	Weak at the federal level, stronger at the state level	Moderate
Political agency	Strong presidential leadership	Strong presidential leadership	Strong commitment of state-level political leaders
Structural features of politics and society			
Institutional depth	Low – history of short-lived constitutions and of military takeover and civil war	Medium – civilian control over military has not always endured, evolving institutions	High – over 50 years of democracy, no threat from the military
Composition of governing elites	Medium to high – historic landed elites are excluded with a new ethnic-regional elite monopolising political appointments	Depends on the state – high concentrations of traditional landed elites in some state governments	Depends on the state – strong landed interests in Karnataka government, less so in Andhra Pradesh

Diversity and depth of civil society	Low – few authoritative apex institutions of labour or capital, and few links to rural civil society	High in places, with effective institutional hosts for the poor	High in most places
Design and implementation variables			
Sequencing, timing and pace of reform	Rapid – strong political commitment, minimal consultation	Gradual – slow, incremental pace of reform, uneven institutional change	Gradual – incremental reform, steady growth of political commitment and public support
Technical capacity	Medium – strong role of elite technocrats in insulated agencies, limited skills in lower levels of bureaucracy	Medium – concentrated in federal ministries	Medium – uneven across ministries and agencies, impetus for reform in specialised arms-length agencies
Devolution to sub-national governments	Low – recent decentralisation, local governments lack capacity	High – many reforms devolved to state level	High – many reforms devolved to state level
Monitorability of reform	Low – little civil society involvement, limited parliamentary scrutiny, weak oversight institutions	Medium – some legislative oversight, limited civil society involvement	High – oversight by state legislatures, civil society organisations and the media

was able to take advantage of the federal political system in Brazil and use his considerable presidential powers to generate support from state governors for gradual, incremental reform and gradually build momentum behind a major policy innovation in the form of the Fiscal Responsibility Law.

Politicians in the south Indian states of Andhra Pradesh and Karnataka have tended to avoid difficult reforms where they anticipated the interests of powerful groups would be adversely affected, and where it was perceived that opposition political parties could gain political mileage from mobilising opposition to reform. Such calculations are especially significant in a context of coalition politics and factional dissent in ruling party blocs under a competitive political system. This helps to explain the limited progress on civil service reform initiatives to date. Conversely, reformist politicians recognise the potential political payoffs that can accrue when large numbers of people benefit from reforms. Improvements in the efficiency of service delivery through institutional reforms in Metro Water in Hyderabad and electronic processing of land records through the *Bhoomi* scheme in Karnataka respectively generate tangible benefits in the form of improved water supplies for large numbers of urban inhabitants and for thousands of farmers who gain from considerably reduced transaction costs, both of which can galvanise political support (Manor, this issue).

By comparison, the extended political tenure of President Museveni under the no-party Movement system in Uganda helped to sustain the momentum of governance reforms and cultivate an expectation that reform momentum would persevere. But, as the Uganda case demonstrates, political longevity can also be counterproductive when a long-established regime seeks to entrench itself politically through the influence of informal institutions based on kinship and ethnicity (Robinson, this issue) and resist further reform that potentially threatens to undermine its support base.

Connections between State and Society

Successful implementation of governance reforms requires political management of potential sources of opposition and resistance through a range of approaches appropriate to the specific prevailing political environment.

Opposition was muted in Uganda by virtue of the no-party political system (in place until July 2005), which limited the scope for political mobilisation by those people adversely affected by the reforms. Trade unions representing government officials were weak and had no organic ties with political parties despite an assured legislative presence. Civil society organisations were not able to mobilise citizens on a large scale or to influence government policy to any significant degree (Robinson & Friedman, 2007). This gave the government considerable room for manoeuvre in managing the reform agenda.

In contrast, reformers in democratic political contexts have to take account of organised opposition to reform. Fragmenting political opposition to reform is a tactic deployed by politicians in the democratic political environments of Brazil and India. This approach was successfully deployed by President Cardoso in the implementation of fiscal reforms in Brazil, in which he persuaded provincial governors to lend their support to the reform process, leading to legislative approval for the initiative. In India, reformist state governments have employed the dual tactics of incremental reform to minimise political opposition and generate public support from reforms that do not threaten vested interests.

The imperatives of democratic politics tend towards more modest and incremental reforms that may have positive, cumulative effects although their overall impact may remain sub-optimal. The experience of Karnataka and Andhra Pradesh suggests that reforms have a much greater chance of success if they do not threaten powerful interest groups or entail the loss of substantial private revenue accruing from rents and public transactions but instead galvanise public support by producing significant improvements for large numbers of people. Minor officials who benefited from side payments from farmers in the manual processing of land records were too dispersed and weakly organised to mount resistance to the *Bhoomi* scheme and opportunities for rent-seeking persisted. The DWRCA program placed increased demands on local officials but did not threaten their job security. But successful reforms of this type that benefit more dispersed, less prosperous and less well-organised rural populations do not provide a durable basis on which support can easily be mobilised unless political parties or civil society groups evince active interest in taking up their cause.

More difficult structural reforms require a combination of incentives and strong leadership to ensure smooth implementation. The implementation of the Ugandan civil service reform programme was facilitated by strong leadership and the creation of incentives in the form of improvements in pay and conditions, and severance benefits funded by aid donors. Organisational restructuring in the form of downsizing and departmental mergers obviated the formation of horizontal alignments among public servants opposed to reform. Weak unions prevented disaffected civil servants from mounting an effective challenge to the reforms. High salaries for employees of the Uganda Revenue Authority acted as a strong incentive for former civil servants in the then Ministry of Finance but those who remained were aggrieved at poor remuneration and managed to erode salary differentials over time.

Incentives are not confined to material benefits in the form of enhanced remuneration. For example, employees in Metro Water and various agencies in the Bangalore municipality responded favourably to positive customer feedback, gaining improved job satisfaction from capacity to respond to citizens' preferences, while increased public appreciation for good performance raised morale.

The policy process remained relatively impermeable to influence from civil society groups in Uganda, and the institutions created to facilitate reform implementation proved incapable of resisting political predation. In this respect, the exclusion of legislators and organised citizens in the process of policy implementation and institutional innovation in the Uganda Revenue Authority weakened oversight and accountability and enabled powerful political interests to subvert reform outcomes. Institutional insulation can provide officials responsible for implementing reforms with a necessary degree of independence from organised interests until the reforms acquire popularity or register some momentum. But without effective oversight and accountability mechanisms through the legislative and judicial machinery, insulation can foster practices that are inimical to sustainability.

Political Agency

The case studies of governance reforms in Brazil, India, and Uganda demonstrate that political agency, defined as the leadership, commitment, and tactics employed by politicians, plays a decisive role in shaping reform outcomes. Political leadership styles varied in the three countries in line with the political context and the nature and significance of forces opposed to reform. Elements common to all three cases were a vision of the potential benefits of reform, strong reliance on government technocrats for reform implementation, and willingness to consider and deliberate a range of reform options.

Strong and consistent political commitment was a contributory factor to successful reform outcomes in all three countries. But it can also have adverse consequences without a conducive political and institutional context in which to exercise it. Uganda's no-party political system is a case in point. The reforms are closely associated with President Museveni who cannot ensure continuity beyond his constitutional tenure with the transition to competitive multi-party politics.[3] Political commitment to reform has waned as more pressing challenges increasingly command the attention of the executive. The Uganda case demonstrates how the imperative of preserving power without widening political support for governance reforms can undermine positive achievements and weaken prospects for sustainability.

A different set of risks for the sustainability of governance reforms arises in competitive political contexts. Experience from the two Indian states demonstrates how a change of government may result in the abandonment of a reform agenda if initiatives are too closely associated with a committed political leader. This risk is greater when reforms emanate from a highly personalised style of decision-making from which opposition political figures may wish to maintain a calculated distance.[4]

The broader economic and political context conditions the feasibility of reform implementation. In particular, post-crisis conditions are an important determinant of the political feasibility of governance reform. This is most readily apparent in Uganda where a dictatorial military regime was ousted through armed struggle and replaced by a reformist government that initially accommodated opposition forces. President Museveni was able to capitalise on popular discontent arising from years of economic mismanagement and state predation in pursuing a sustained governance reform agenda. In Brazil, gradual fiscal reforms that culminated in the Fiscal Responsibility Law were made possible by the severity of the financial crisis that persuaded recalcitrant politicians of the need for a new policy framework. In contrast, the fiscal crisis made the federal government less willing to radically reform the tax system, as it became nervous about the prospective loss of revenues through more progressive tax legislation.

Institutional Depth

The longevity, flexibility, and adaptability of formal and informal institutions shape the process of bargaining between social groups and the means by which losers from reforms are compensated. Some reforms occur within the boundaries of existing institutions, which can produce significant results, but without any change in the underlying pact or rules of the game. Actors adapt at the margins to changing circumstances but do not modify the terms of the pact. Other reforms entail wholesale institutional change in which one set of institutions displaces another on the basis of a new pact between interested actors. Wholesale institutional change can be driven by external factors such as economic crisis or institutional decay. This framework is invoked to explain differential reform outcomes in tax reform and the Fiscal Responsibility Law in Brazil.[5] Wholesale institutional change did occur in Uganda but without the creation of pacts that helped to ensure reform implementation in Brazil. Incremental change in India generally operated within the boundaries of existing institutions and did not fundamentally alter the rules of the game.

Informal institutions have a significant bearing on the implementation of governance reforms in all three countries under review, in terms of their scope, timing, and longevity. In Brazil these take the form of patronage emanating from clientelist politics, reflected in pressure on politicians and policy-makers to make public expenditure decisions in line with reciprocal expectations of political support. Informal institutions in India that influence governance outcomes are largely grounded in political culture and the personal agendas of political leaders, in which bargaining and accommodation are key features of a strategic political calculus employed by politicians in a democratic political context. Traditional institutions founded on caste and religion did not play an overt role in shaping the implementation of governance reforms in India, even though they are fundamental to strategic decisions in many other policy spheres. Successful governance reforms in the two Indian states engaged stakeholders as citizens and clients rather than through an appeal to parochial considerations, which may help to mitigate the influence of informal institutions. In Uganda, by comparison, kinship, family, and ascriptive affinities were gradually reasserted during the process of governance reform, in which fresh opportunities for patronage and rent-seeking emerged through the creation or reorganisation of formal institutions in the public sector, such as the semi-autonomous revenue authority and specialised agencies and commissions in the civil service.

The longevity of political and bureaucratic institutions has a direct bearing on successful implementation. Stable and long-established institutions are often associated with credibility and predictability, even if they are subject to deficiencies. Democratic political institutions function in this manner in India and have proved capable of accommodating both new entrants to the political system and dissent, which simplifies the task of reformist politicians. Formal institutions place boundaries on the behaviour of elected politicians and bureaucrats, who are forced to bargain and compromise over the design of governance reforms, within a set of widely accepted and well-entrenched political rules and norms. Politicians in Karnataka and Andhra Pradesh thus pursued reform strategies that minimised the potential threat to vested interests, limited the scope for derailment by the opposition, and produced visible benefits for large numbers of people.

Insulation of policy-makers and the institutions responsible for policy implementation from politicians and the political influence of organised interests is often a key design premise in governance reform strategies. Several cases of successful reforms rest on the formation of independent implementing agencies or autonomous enclave authorities in Uganda and other countries in Africa for the purpose of tax administration and civil service reforms. But the assumption that insulation provides effective protection from predatory political interests and lobby groups does not hold up to empirical scrutiny in Uganda, since autonomous agencies remain subject to executive interference in the absence of political accountability and an independent governance structure. In India, by comparison, politicians initiated reforms through institutional innovations that were relatively insulated from societal influence and short-term political pressure. Once the reforms gained momentum and produced visible benefits, the political process became more open to influence from civil society, making policy reversal by opposition politicians more difficult to achieve.

Composition of Governing Elites

The conceptual framework draws attention to change in the composition of ruling elites and the formation of durable pacts between major interest groups as a possible factor influencing reform outcomes. In particular, the expectation is that traditional elites will resist reform efforts and the formation of pro-reform coalitions where these are perceived to have the potential to challenge power relations founded on clientelist politics. In practice, however, elite resistance was not a significant factor in explaining the trajectory of reform implementation in the case studies.

Although reformist governments in Karnataka and Andhra Pradesh attracted the support of urban business and professional elites, governance reforms did not generate resistance from landed interests. Rural elites in India were not threatened by the computerisation of land records, since it did not affect their asset holdings, or the formation of self-help groups through the DWCRA programme, as these remained under elite influence. Policy and bureaucratic elites became more diverse as a result of private sector involvement in the BATF and the recruitment of management specialists by Metro Water, in the process eroding the dominance of public sector bureaucratic and technical elites, but without provoking a backlash from these interests.

In Brazil there was partial challenge to the power of traditional elites who benefited from political patronage under past regimes. The Fiscal Responsibility Law altered the relationship between sub-national governments and the central government in a significant way, in particular by ending bailouts of state debts. This provides support for the proposition that the composition of the governing elite and special interest groups with access to these elites will affect the willingness of politicians to undertake reform. In this respect, the political coalition that supported reforms to the federal system was not sufficient to mount a more fundamental and structural challenge to traditional elites through tax reform, and had to be satisfied with marginal changes and sub-optimal outcomes.

Governance reforms in Uganda posed a threat to vested bureaucratic interests that profited from rents and corrupt practices but provoked little overt opposition from this quarter. In part, this reflected the limited scope to mobilise political opposition to the reforms or for trade unions to represent disaffected civil servants. Dissent was also mitigated by voluntary severance, pay reform, and the creation of sinecures for top civil servants in specialised government agencies. But the lack of opposition also arose from the displacement of traditional governing elites from political power by the Movement regime, infusing the reform process with greater autonomy from vested interests.

Diversity and Depth of Civil Society

The diversity and depth of civil society and its capacity to respond positively to reforms is a further explanatory factor in successful reform outcomes. The extent of involvement of non-state actors varied considerably in India and Brazil and would appear to be largely dependent on the nature of the reform process. Policy-makers concerned with public management reforms in Brazil did not establish durable alliances with groups outside the state but established pacts with organised interests as a means of ensuring the progressive implementation of reform objectives. This may reflect the technical content of the reform initiatives and the perception that there would be little to be gained from opening up the reform process to powerful interests that could subvert reform outcomes. In India there was limited engagement of civil society in the design of reform initiatives but a gradual opening up to influence from below in the process of implementation, which helped to broaden support for the reforms. These experiences lead to the proposition that in democratic contexts where reforms are politically contentious a more inclusive process of policy design could invite insurmountable opposition at an early stage of implementation and undermine the success of the initiative.

Citizen engagement in governance reform processes is expected to be greater when there is higher literacy and an active and diverse media. The case study evidence from India provides some support for this contention. Although civil society organisations did not play a significant role in the *Bhoomi* scheme or Metro Water, representatives from prominent NGOs and the private sector in Bangalore assumed a leading role in the BATF and in the design of its various reform initiatives. The BATF also created an opportunity for citizens to exercise some voice and influence in the policy process, in the form of publicity campaigns, consumer surveys, and other participatory devices, attracting considerable media attention in the process. The DWCRA groups are not autonomous civil society organisations but rather can be considered as government sponsored. Despite the lack of organisational autonomy they were able to channel popular preferences and influence politics and the policy process. Three of the Indian state government initiatives actively sought to catalyse participation by ordinary people, either as clients who could demand better service standards, or as citizens empowered through local organisations to assume a more active role in negotiating with state institutions in their localities. Mobilisation of civil society facilitated greater access to the policy process and generated support from people who were previously disaffected with or apathetic towards the state administration.

The Ugandan and Brazilian cases offer a contrasting set of insights in this regard. In Uganda, civil society has not featured as a significant force in the implementation of the governance reforms reviewed for this study, with the possible exception of anti-corruption where some organisations heightened public awareness on the extent and pervasiveness of the problem though national integrity surveys. However, these did not directly affect the design of anti-corruption institutions established for this purpose. The absence of significant civil society involvement in monitoring the activities and performance of these institutions is a factor in their inability to significantly reduce corruption in the public service. Reforms in fiscal management in Brazil were also characterised by a lack of civil society involvement in implementation, and were essentially an outcome of negotiated pacts between politicians at different levels of government.

Sequencing, Timing and Pace of Reform

Factors related to political support and the preservation of political power influence the timing and sequencing of governance reforms. Democratic politics invariably fosters an incremental approach to reform in which governments introduce reforms in a gradual manner, partly to limit damaging reactions and to slowly build up support for reform initiatives. Cumulative reform initiatives that do not threaten the interests of powerful groups but benefit large numbers of people can have a significant impact on governance outcomes, as demonstrated by the experience of the two south Indian states. Incremental changes introduced by reform initiatives in Karnataka and Andhra Pradesh produced a cumulative effect in which the broader system of governance became more open, transparent, and responsive to popular influence over the policy process.

An incremental approach is also consistent with the formation of pacts between reformers and key stakeholders, which provides a more durable political basis for reform. The Fiscal Responsibility Law in Brazil illustrates the success of an incremental approach in which a series of small, mutually reinforcing fiscal reform measures culminated in a significant institutional innovation that has the potential for a major improvement in public financial management. The incremental process leading to legislation had the effect of gradually strengthening supporters in the federal government and weakening its opponents in state governments over the course of a decade until a threshold was reached in which a new pact was formed around public finances and federal relations.

However, incrementalism can impede more fundamental reforms by operating within the parameters of existing institutions, and give rise to modest outcomes that do not produce deeper structural change. This is evident from the example of Brazilian tax reforms, which increased tax revenues but did not challenge the regressive and inefficient character of the tax system. Attempts to forge new pacts among interested actors were unsuccessful, which meant that the federal government relied on incremental changes in existing institutions to raise revenues in the absence of fundamental policy change.

An incremental approach may also deflect attention from more difficult and intractable reforms. The reluctance of reformers in India and some Latin American countries to pursue structural reforms in the bureaucracy on account of potential political resistance highlights the limits to incremental approaches when politicians fail to recognise that improvements in bureaucratic capacity and erosion of rent-seeking opportunities will produce enduring benefits for ordinary citizens.

A more rapid approach to reform implementation can generate successful outcomes under two contrasting sets of conditions. In Uganda considerable time was given to the design of civil service reforms to build political support and strengthen technical capacity, while the various elements of the reform package were implemented relatively quickly. Careful preparation of the civil service restructuring exercise through a special presidential commission led to a series of well-planned reforms that were implemented in rapid succession. A similar pattern was evident in the case of the Uganda Revenue Authority, with an extended period of preparation followed by rapid implementation. The two rural reform initiatives in India were also rolled out quickly, to cultivate popular support and to ensure substantial uptake. The lack of opposition to the reforms and the potential to actively cultivate public support through the reform process made speedy implementation possible.

These cases lead to the conclusion that incremental approaches work well when there is potential opposition to reform and pacts need to be negotiated to ensure successful implementation. Conversely, rapid implementation is possible where vested interests are not threatened or where a top-down process will not be challenged politically. In such cases, more ambitious governance reforms may be possible in the short term, provided that attention is given to broadening political and public support for reform during the course of implementation.

Technical Capacity

High-level technical capacity was evident in most cases of successful governance reform in all three review cases, heightening government ownership of the initiatives, even though implementation capacity was more limited at lower levels. In Brazil and Uganda economists in the respective ministries of finance were key actors, applying sound technical criteria in the design of fiscal and public sector management reforms. Technocrats in the Bangalore municipal corporation worked in close cooperation with private sector representatives in the BATF to produce policy prescriptions for municipal reform. Some reform initiatives drew on particular forms of technical expertise in their design, such as the *Bhoomi* scheme in Karnataka that relied on information technology specialists in the computerisation of land records, but once the infrastructure was in place implementation could be assigned to non-technical administrators. In the case of Metro Water the involvement of managers and specialists in designing a more customer-oriented approach proved much more effective than the traditional top-down approaches favoured by engineers who had earlier predominated among technical staff in the organisation.

Similarly, generally low levels of donor funding also increased government ownership of the various initiatives. It was only in Uganda that reforms relied heavily on funding and some technical assistance from external sources.

Devolution to Sub-national Governments

The literature on economic reform assumes that devolution of responsibility for some reforms to lower levels of government deflects some of the opposition to reform and potentially broadens the gains from it. There is some evidence in support of this claim from the fiscal reform programme in Brazil, where budgetary reforms successively negotiated with state governments eventually had a major bearing on reform implementation and outcomes at the federal level. The federal government had to persuade state governors to subscribe to a fiscal reform agenda, but this tier of government did not assume a lead role in driving fiscal reform efforts since it challenged the vested interests that had built up around high levels of fiscal autonomy in the states. The dependence of congressional representatives at the federal level on support from state-level politicians meant that it was not easy for reformist agendas devised at the federal level to find support until there was a change in political leadership following profound fiscal crisis.

While the case studies did not examine decentralisation initiatives as such, some of the reform initiatives in India were implemented at the state and municipal level, with differing levels of engagement on the part of local administrations. This relates to the contention in the conceptual framework that the pursuit of governance reforms at a sub-national level can open up space for experimentation with reform which in turn encourages other jurisdictions to follow a similar path.[6] Similarly, state governments in Karnataka and Andhra Pradesh have assumed the lead in governance reforms and in some cases have registered greater success than the national government. The elected municipal administration in Bangalore had sufficient autonomy to experiment with new forms of municipal service provision through the BATF, which had both private sector and NGO representation, but this did not have a significant bearing on the design and outcome of this reform initiative as BATF was just one of seven municipal agencies that were involved in the experiment. The Metro Water reform programme in the city of Hyderabad was implemented without significant involvement on the part of the municipal council. The two rural initiatives in India were both top-down and did not operate through elected local councils. In Karnataka this reflected the technical design features of the *Bhoomi* scheme, which was centred on computer kiosks at the sub-district level in which local councils did not play a significant role, whereas in Andhra Pradesh the decision to promote DWCRA groups as an alternative to local councils where the ruling party lacked a strong power base was politically motivated. While the Indian case studies provide some evidence to support the contention that working at the local level will entail closer civil society involvement in governance reform and improve accountability and the quality of implementation, it was not possible to draw firm conclusions from the limited number of case studies.[7]

'Monitorability' of Reform

The openness of governance reforms to public scrutiny and legislative oversight is often taken to be a factor in promoting greater government commitment and improved sustainability of the reform process. Yet the case material provides limited evidence in support of this contention. In general the types of governance reforms examined in the cases were often insulated from legislative oversight and difficult for independent groups to monitor. Legislative involvement was especially limited in the Ugandan case and there were few opportunities for public engagement and oversight in the reform process. While there was civil society and media engagement in surveying the form and extent of corruption there was limited scope for direct involvement in the creation and operation of specialised anti-corruption agencies designed to tackle the problem. Similarly the federal and state legislatures in Brazil did not play an active role in overseeing the design and implementation of the reform agenda, which largely resulted from executive action on the part of the President. By their very nature taxation and financial management reforms are technically complex and not amenable to engagement by legislators or civil society organisations. In India the reforms were more conducive to civil society and legislative engagement as they focused on service delivery, which had the potential to generate tangible benefits for citizens. This was most evident in the case of the BATF, which provided a platform for monitoring government performance by civil society organisations but did not actively cultivate the involvement of municipal councillors, leading to political marginalisation of this initiative following a change in government. As governance reforms are often relatively impervious to external monitoring, by virtue of their relative insulation and technical complexity, this limits the scope to build and sustain reform commitment through external pressure and oversight.

Key Explanatory Variables

The case studies from Brazil, India, and Uganda provide detailed insights into governance reform trajectories in a range of country and regime contexts and highlight the conditions that give rise to successful implementation. The findings suggest that three key political and institutional variables are common to successful governance reforms: the extent of political commitment; the degree of technical capacity and insulation; and the timing and sequencing of reform measures.[8] Similar conclusions arise from Levy's review of initiatives designed to strengthen state capacity in sub-Saharan Africa, in which political commitment and incremental approaches emerge as critical ingredients of successful reforms (Levy, this issue).

Political commitment

Political commitment at the highest level of government is a critical factor in initiating and sustaining governance reforms.[9] Visible commitment from the top political leadership supports officials responsible for implementation, and guards against opposition from those who might suffer from the reforms. In democratic settings, the decision to embark on reform is motivated by a shrewd assessment of the potential political costs and benefits, and strategies designed to manage and accommodate informal institutions centred on patronage and rent-seeking. Democratic regimes tend towards incremental approaches to reform in order to minimise potential opposition. Initial reforms may be modest but there is recognition that the cumulative effect of small changes may generate political dividends from improved outcomes. Governments in non-democratic settings are able to introduce more challenging reforms as they are able to mitigate political opposition and contain challenges from those adversely affected by the reforms. However, a lack of political accountability combined with the imperative of maintaining political power can subvert the longer-term sustainability of governance reforms.

Technical capacity and insulation

A high degree of technical capacity is a common feature of successful reform. Such capacity may be concentrated in particular ministries and agencies and may take time to cultivate and develop. The infusion of new types of technical and managerial skills into organisations dominated by traditional civil servants or sector specialists can foster experimentation with new approaches. Insulation of policy-makers and technocrats from societal and political pressure provides a sound basis for institutional design at the inception stage, but the exclusion of organised interests during implementation is not conducive to democratic accountability or the effectiveness and sustainability of reforms. Excessive insulation limits scope for independent oversight and creates opportunities for rent-seeking and patronage, which can stall or reverse reforms. Initial insulation followed by gradual opening-up of the policy process during the course of implementation appears to be more conducive to sustainable outcomes.

Timing and sequencing

The findings indicate that some categories of governance reform are easier to achieve than others. Incremental reforms that are carefully selected to minimise opposition and produce modest initial benefits have a greater chance of success and sustainability than wholesale reforms that are implemented relatively quickly.[10] The former include innovations in service delivery and institutional reforms designed to improve civil service accountability. These do not entail zero-sum games in that the benefits resulting from improved delivery of services can generate popular support and embolden reformers, as a means of offsetting opposition from bureaucrats and politicians who stand to lose power and influence. Bureaucrats also benefit from positive reactions from citizens who receive better services, elevating their status and job satisfaction, thereby fostering commitment to reform.

Reforms that require structural changes in fiscal management, tax administration, and civil service organisation are more difficult to accomplish. Political commitment and material incentives to buy off potential opposition are important contributory factors but sustainability is hard to achieve in the absence of visible results that secure wider political support and public approval. Reforms that entail wholesale institutional change can be accomplished in two ways: through a gradual, cumulative set of reforms that give rise to significant change, or through the absence of a direct threat to bureaucratic or societal interests who are in a position to block or derail reform initiatives.

Wider Implications

This final section considers the wider significance of the case studies for analytical and operational work in governments and donor agencies that have an interest in promoting and supporting governance reform efforts. It can inform those responsible for designing, implementing, and financing governance reforms on how to recognise and implement the political and institutional factors conducive to success and identify what options exist for aid donors when those factors are either absent or in short supply.

Both the case studies and broader operational experience highlight the fundamental importance of domestic political commitment to successful reform outcomes. In the absence of positive incentives, aid donors can make little headway in persuading politicians and government officials of the virtues of reform, especially when the financial significance of external support is relatively modest. Many well-designed governance reform programmes have foundered in the absence of political support, with the result that the potential benefits are not realised, opposition is mobilised, and the scope for further reform is deferred. The main impetus for reform will come from politicians who recognise that the potential benefits can outweigh the risks, and that opponents to reform can be countered and out-manoeuvred without significant threat to their continued incumbency.

Political risk can be mitigated by careful attention to design considerations and the timing and sequencing of reforms. Incremental reforms that involve small, cumulative changes are unlikely to provoke significant opposition from traditional elites; such reforms can build public support and in turn fortify political leaders, and can combine to achieve larger-scale impacts over time. Incremental reforms can also be mutually reinforcing: innovations in service delivery can produce efficiency gains as well as improvements in accountability, while measures designed to combat corruption can increase the quality of spending on public services by reducing leakages. The political advantages of an incremental approach do not obviate the case for complex structural reforms involving the reorganisation or creation of new public agencies. Rather, they highlight the need for an extended preparatory process in which core capacities are strengthened and measures to compensate losers from reforms are built into programme design.

A further implication of the case study research relates to the political benefits of longer time horizons. This may entail a trade-off between the speed of reform and its effectiveness and sustainability. An incremental approach fostered by a pragmatic political leadership that builds a domestic constituency for reform in a competitive political environment requires a longer-term time horizon. Recent public sector governance projects in Africa consisting in cumulative and phased policy innovations and reforms over a more extended period of time (in some cases up to a decade) are indicative of this trend.[11] A more gradual approach may be sub-optimal in terms of achieving quick results but may ensure more sustainable implementation with the potential for cumulative impact.

The fact that the successful implementation of governance reforms is predicated on reservoirs of technical capacity within the organisation responsible for managing the reform process presents something of a paradox. On the one hand, successful governance reforms require high-calibre technical leadership but the acquisition of the necessary skills and resources can take time and may require external support. Technical assistance cannot promote reform in the absence of political commitment and strong domestic ownership of the reform process.

Governance reforms are characterised by an inherent tension between institutional insulation and a political impetus toward wider participation in policy-making. The case studies caution against excessive consultation in the design and early phases of implementation of governance reforms. Widespread consultation can allow political opponents to mobilise opposition and self-interested civil society actors to maximise their influence to the detriment of reform implementation. Gradual opening up of reform implementation to wider involvement and creating channels for citizen feedback and influence is a more effective way of building support, especially where the emphasis is on improved service delivery, as citizens can see the benefits of reform and exert pressure for further change.

However, effective oversight and monitoring mechanisms are required at an early stage of reform to mitigate opportunities for rent-seeking arising from new institutional arrangements, such as semi-autonomous tax authorities, or to prevent specialised institutions like anti-corruption agencies from being neutralised by the political opposition. But some types of reform may not be amenable to wider consultation on account of their technical complexity. Efforts to broaden public consultation in governance reform efforts should therefore be informed by a careful assessment of the potential trade-offs between improved accountability and potential losses in efficiency.

These considerations raise a series of operational implications for aid donors seeking to promote and finance governance reforms. First, there is a need to recognise that successful governance reform agendas are domestically driven and emanate from clear and unambiguous political commitment. Second, support for incremental reform is more likely to prove rewarding over the longer term than time-bound reform initiatives that promote major structural changes in prevailing incentive systems. This highlights the value of modest financial outlays which have the potential for scaling-up over time, supported by flexible lending instruments that respond to new opportunities for reform and build on cumulative interventions. Third, and by extension, financial outlays are more likely to take the form of selective infusions of technical assistance where capacity is limited or requires strengthening, or where resources are needed for compensation packages for losers from reform processes.

Donors seeking to promote reform must pay close attention to the political feasibility of reform, helping to identify and build incentives for reform, and working with reform-oriented politicians and bureaucrats would be a more fruitful approach. While this approach might be less appealing to proponents of more concerted engagement and greater resource intensity, the experience of failed governance reform efforts in the past is a salutary reminder of the virtues of incrementalism and small-scale, flexible responses to domestically driven reform agendas.

Notes

1. The role of aid donors in the design, financing, and implementation of governance reforms is not explicitly examined in this article, which focuses on key elements of the domestic political and institutional environment in shaping successful design and implementation. Aid donors only played a significant role in contributing to the financing and design of reforms in Uganda, whereas in Brazil and India the impetus for reform came principally from domestic governments.
2. The reforms reviewed here do not include those with explicit political and normative objectives pertaining to the legitimate exercise of political power and the promotion of social justice. The rationale for the selection of the case studies and an account of the wider policy environment prevailing in each country or state (sub-national jurisdictions in India) is set out in the individual papers in this issue.
3. The constitutional term limit of two presidential terms was lifted through a parliamentary vote in June 2005. President Museveni won the multi-party presidential elections in July 2005, which extends his term of office for a further four years.
4. The abandonment of many of the reform initiatives associated with Chandrababu Naidu, the former Chief Minister of Andhra Pradesh, by his successor is illustrative of this point.
5. A fuller exploration of the utility of this approach in explaining reform outcomes is not possible within the scope of this article. For details of this approach see Schneider, this issue.
6. This is certainly the case with governance reforms in various Brazilian states, which have made fiscal reform initiatives at the federal level more palatable and politically less contentious.
7. Establishing the veracity of this claim would require more concentration on decentralisation and local administration as the focal point of governance reform efforts, or a comparative study of governance reforms in sub-national units, such as state-level jurisdictions in Brazil and India.
8. Other variables also played a role in successful implementation, such as the choice of instruments for implementing organisational change and mechanisms for strengthening accountability, but these applied unevenly across the cases reviewed here.
9. A review of 25 cases of successful public service delivery reforms in India arrived at the same conclusion, namely the centrality of political leadership in initiating and sustaining reforms (World Bank, 2006).
10. Levy comes to a similar conclusion in his review of lessons from successful state capacity-building initiatives in Africa: 'Rather than remaining preoccupied with politically unachievable comprehensive reforms, the focus is on more modest, viable initiatives, especially those for which results are observable.' (Levy, 2004: 28).
11. For example, see Levy and Kpundeh (2004) and Kiragu and Mukandala (2005).

References

Campos, J. E. & Pradhan, S. (2005) A framework for studying governance reforms at the country level, in *Economic Growth in the 1990s: Learning from a Decade of Reform* (Washington DC: World Bank).

Goetz, A. M. (2007) Manoeuvring past clientelism: institutions and incentives to generate constituencies in support of governance reforms, *Commonwealth and Comparative Politics*, 45(4), pp. 403–424.

Kiragu, K. & Mukandala, R. (2005) *Politics and Tactics in Public Sector Reforms: The Dynamics of Public Service Pay in Africa* (Dar es Salaam: Dar es Salaam University Press).

Levy, B. (2004) Governance and economic development in Africa: meeting the challenge of capacity building, in B. Levy & S .Kpundeh (Eds) *Building State Capacity in Africa: New Approaches, Emerging Lessons* (Washington, DC: World Bank), 1–43.

Levy, B. & Kpundeh, S. (Eds) (2004) *Building State Capacity in Africa: New Approaches, Emerging Lessons* (Washington, DC: World Bank).

Manor, J. (2007) Successful governance reforms in two Indian states: Karnataka and Andhra Pradesh, *Commonwealth and Comparative Politics*, 45(4), pp. 425–451.

Robinson, M. (2007) The political economy of governance reforms in Uganda, *Commonwealth and Comparative Politics*, 45(4), pp. 452–474.

Robinson, M. & Friedman, S. (2007) Civil society, democratization and foreign aid: civic engagement and public policy in South Africa and Uganda, *Democratization*, 14(4), pp. 1–27.

Schneider, A. (2007) Governance reform and institutional change in Brazil: federalism and tax, *Commonwealth and Comparative Politics*, 45(4), pp. 475–498.

World Bank (2006) *Reforming Public Services in India: Drawing Lessons from Success* (New Delhi, Thousand Oaks and London: Sage Publications).

INDEX